# The Food Economy

# The Food Economy

## Global issues and challenges

edited by:

**Frank Bunte**
**Hans Dagevos**

*Wageningen Academic*
*P u b l i s h e r s*

ISBN 978-90-8686-109-5

Cover design: Marjolein de Vette

First published, 2009

© Wageningen Academic Publishers
The Netherlands, 2009

# Table of contents

Preface                                                                      11
  *Gérard Viatte*

**Part 1 – Introduction**

Expanding the size of the envelope that contains agriculture    15
  *Hans Dagevos and Frank Bunte*

**Part 2 – Market structures, mechanisms and materials**

Globalisation in the food industry: the impact on market
structures and firm postures                                                 23
  *Arjen van Witteloostuijn*

The food economy of today and tomorrow                                       43
  *Frank Bunte*

The biofuels boom: implications for world food markets                       61
  *Dileep K. Birur, Thomas W. Hertel and Wallace E. Tyner*

**Part 3 – 'Software' becoming 'hardware'**

Informing consumers about social and environmental
conditions of globalised production                                          79
  *Barbara Fliess*

The interplay between private and public food safety standards 99
  *Pepijn van de Port*

Making the livestock sector more sustainable                                109
  *Henning Steinfeld*

## Part 4 – Perspectives on food policy

Food policy in practice: the case of France     123
  *Egizio Valceschini*

In response to challenges: Canada's agriculture and agri-
food policy evolution     135
  *Tulay Yildirim and Margaret Zafiriou*

Food for thought: setting the food policy's research agenda     153
  *Loek Boonekamp, Bruce Lee and Hans Dagevos*

## Part 5 – Conclusion

Anticipating the future of the food economy     165
  *Frank Bunte and Hans Dagevos*

References     181

Contributors     191

# Preface

In today's society, a new food economy is emerging, and it has very different characteristics from those at the end of the previous century. For a long time, it was been recognised that the agricultural sector was only part of the food economy and that it had to be seen within the context of the food supply chain, including activities from upstream to downstream. However, this supply chain concept is not sufficient today. The new food economy is characterised by its holistic nature, as it is at the centre of major global societal concerns.

One of the key political issues is food safety. More generally, food is now a major element in relation to general health concerns. Food is also linked to the general objective of long-term sustainability, from the production and consumption viewpoints – discussions about 'food miles' and ecological 'foodprints' show that the issue is not just theoretical. More broadly, food has always had cultural aspects: the concept of 'slow food' is an interesting case. Ethical considerations and concerns have become more evident and more widespread in the context of the current information age.

These developments and dimensions do not mean that the economic aspects of the food system have become less relevant. On the contrary, various developments including technological change or the demand for organic food contribute to a more diversified food economy with a variety of producers and marketing channels. In the global food economy, competition is more acute than ever. Within this context, globalisation and regionalisation develop in parallel, leaving scope for both mass and niche products. Trade flows become more complex, even though liberalisation in agricultural and food products is still limited by various trade obstacles, which create particular problems for developing countries. Foreign Direct Investment is also a powerful tool for globalisation.

These new dimensions of the food economy create challenges for policy makers, at both national and international levels. The concept of food policy must therefore be addressed. Food policy has been developed in a systematic and comprehensive manner in some countries, whereas in others it has not been clearly articulated. In all cases, the new dimensions of the food economy require more coherence among the numerous policies involved, far beyond the 'classical' agricultural and trade policies. Governments and the private sector also need to develop new relations, and new types of partnerships – as evidenced in the case of standards.

The above-mentioned issues and challenges receive full attention in the present publication. This book has its origins in the Conference 'The Future of the Food Economy' organised by the OECD Directorate for Trade and Agriculture, the Dutch Ministry of Agriculture, Nature and Food Quality, and the Dutch Agricultural Economics Research Institute (LEI Wageningen UR) in October 2007 in The Hague. Hopefully, *The Food Economy* will help to widen the audience and the scope of the debate in which new developments and unexpected changes in the food economy are discussed. In the international and 'multi-stakeholder' context, which was well reflected in the Conference, it is increasingly important to identify future orientations for action by the public and the private sector, as well for economic and social research. There is a permanent need for various forums to review these changes and to discuss jointly effective responses, which represent a challenge for all actors, including all of us as consumers. Today's economic slow-down provides ample reason to reflect upon the present and future challenges and what action they require. So, keep on discussing the dynamics in the food economy!

*Gérard Viatte*
*Chairman of the Future of the Food Economy Conference*

# Part 1

# Introduction

# Expanding the size of the envelope that contains agriculture

*Hans Dagevos and Frank Bunte*

> *As the food economy develops, the impacts reverberate far and wide.* – (Southgate *et al.*, 2007: 3)

In his best selling book, *Fast Food Nation*, the American journalist Eric Schlosser notes that '[w]hat we eat has changed more in the last forty years than in the previous forty thousand' (Schlosser, 2001: 7). However drastic the changes in the food products we can find today in supermarkets, speciality shops or restaurants, they embody as a matter of fact the radical and continuous changes behind the scenes – i.e. transformations in the food system which take place largely hidden from the consumers' view. Maybe it is because of the tremendous dynamics in the modern food system in recent decades that – in the wake of Schlosser's *Fast Food Nation* – a stream of books has been published recently which critically reflect upon the current food world in general and its prevalent production practices, marketing strategies or power and organisational structures in particular (see e.g. Korthals, 2004; Lang and Heasman, 2004; Lawrence, 2004, 2008; Patel, 2007; Petrini, 2007; Pollan, 2006, 2008; Singer and Mason, 2006; Weis, 2007).

Whatever the differences between these studies, next to their critical stance, the common factor in this literature is that it aims to contribute to consumer awareness, or even activism, with respect to the food we eat and the choices we make. In a way, it tries to make a contribution to bridging the gap that has grown between food production and consumption. However, it is rightly claimed that 'rebuilding connections between producers and consumers is a challenging and difficult task' (Wilk, 2006: 22).

In large parts of the present-day world we face the paradoxical situation that while the availability and accessibility of a wide variety of food products as well as food outlets are unprecedented, ordinary people simultaneously are alienated from their food. The latter because the food system has become ever less visible and comprehensible to consumers. On the one hand, people in (post-)modern service economies are largely disconnected from farmers and farms as well as from plants and animals. On the other hand, major drivers in the world's food system also keep end users at a distance. Nowadays, the production and processing of foodstuffs is industrialised to such levels of sophistication that such processes and practices are hardly understandable to laymen. Moreover, all this takes place behind the concrete walls of laboratories, slaughterhouses and factories located

*We face the paradoxical situation that while the availability and accessibility of a wide variety of food products as well as food outlets are unprecedented, ordinary people simultaneously are alienated from their food*

far away from the living environment of most people or in other parts of the globe. Power concentration in the food system means that anonymous trans-national companies provide anonymous consumers worldwide with anonymous food products – or its composite parts – from all over the planet. Food advertisements and product labels not only result in transparency but also frequently confuse food consumers. In other words, basic trends in the food system such as industrialisation, globalisation, commodification and innovation easily reinforce rather than reduce both the physical and psychological distance between producers and consumers.

## The food system as a continuum

Regarding producers and consumers as remote emphasises a gap between the two ends of the agri-food supply chain. This viewpoint accords with the idea of the contemporary food system that features bipolarities. That is, a variety of interlinked bidirectional tendencies and binary notions seem to be characteristic of the present-day world of food. For instance, the globalisation and homogenisation of dietary patterns as well as the promotion of global food brands go hand in hand with heterogeneous regional food product initiatives and innovative localised consumption infrastructures. The alleged opposing spheres of 'self-interested' consumers and 'public-oriented' citizens turn out to be overlapping domains rather than different and distinctive by definition. Fast food structures aiming at heavily standardised commodity production, predictability and efficiency form part of the food system as well as slow food structures emphasising food quality conventions based on craftsmanship and authenticity. A corresponding dichotomy of 'mass food' and 'class food' – put crudely: hamburgers vs. haute cuisine – is represented by the presence of both high-tech food production processes and organic production chains – or, to put it in the vocabulary of Tim Lang and Michael Heasman: the simultaneous emergence of two new paradigms of food supply, which are coined respectively the life sciences integrated paradigm 'that has at its core a mechanistic and fairly medicalised interpretation of human and environmental health', and the ecologically integrated paradigm that 'takes a more integrative and less engineering approach to nature' (Lang and Heasman, 2004: 22; 26).

*A variety of interlinked bidirectional tendencies and binary notions seem to be characteristic of the present-day world of food*

It is possible to continue by pointing at a bidirectional trend in which contemporary food consumers prove to be indifferent and ignorant as to the way food is produced but at the same time express their involvement, concerns and anxieties with respect to what they eat and the ways their food is produced. From the supplier side, it is evident that agribusinesses are not exclusively occupied with rising sales and profit figures, but also respond to public concerns by developing private responsibilities in reaction or in addition to public requirements. Another contrast at the supply side can be observed in product standardisation and efficiency that are reflected in industry concentration on the one hand and the slicing up of the supply chain on the other.

We can also witness the contradictory fact that the rising consumer interest in healthy foods is keeping pace with a rising prevalence in overweight and obesity. Even more topical is the poignant contradiction between scarcity, hunger and malnutrition in the least developed regions of the globe and the ever growing abundance and affluence in other parts of the world. This striking contrast is reinforced by the use of agricultural raw commodities for non-food applications, bio-fuels in particular. In the international policy arena, the contradiction between scarcity and abundance is reflected in the ongoing protection of the wealthy and the powerful to the detriment of the poor and the powerless, according to Joseph Stiglitz (2006). Expectations diverge with respect to the question of whether a Doha agreement is able to create a level playing field for the least developing countries. Finally, it is also possible to point to the fact that despite the dynamism and diversity of today's food market, we should not lose sight of the fact that next to change and variety stability and (the power of) habits are still important catchwords. So, it is still relevant to talk about conventions, traditions and patterns in the field of food production and consumption.

To argue that antagonistic trends and polar notions are typical of the modern world of food implies an emphasis, rather than a denial of the fact that all kinds of counter currents and opposites are interconnected and exist and evolve simultaneously. For this reason, it is wise to bear in mind that binary contrasts must be treated as two poles of a continuum rather than being discussed in zero-sum terms. As a consequence, this perspective takes the word system seriously in its definition as a set of different elements or parts that hang together. The food system, then, consists of a wide variety of interrelated agents and inextricably interwoven phenomena that influence each other. Moreover, we argue that the scope of the food system is expanding. It is in this light that the present book may be seen.

## A broad view and our focal points

We believe that a broad view is required if one aims to look at issues and challenges which are important to today's and tomorrow's food system. This conviction corresponds to Jean Kinsey's comprehensive perspective when she coined the notion of 'New Food Economy'. Kinsey (2001) argues persuasively that it is important to approach the food arena with broad definitions of agriculture and a willingness to reflect upon the entire food chain. For this reason, we choose to take a phrase of Kinsey as the title of this introductory chapter. 'Expanding the size of the envelope that contains agriculture' expresses in flowery language what is a guiding principle for this book.

In recognising that the food system is multidimensional and ranges from global to local, from farm to fork, from McDonald's to Michelin gourmet restaurants, from scientific laboratories to supermarket shelves, and that it includes a variety of agents ('financial sector, labour unions, governmental agencies, and educational institutions', to name just a few that Kinsey (2001: 1114) mentions) and issues ('natural resource and environmental issues, labour and marketing practices, waste disposal and recycling practices, and public policies that are important to participating firms, consumers, citizens and even tourists', to cite Kinsey again), it is all the more clear that it is by no means our intention to present a complete picture in this volume. We have made a selection of topics that we think are important to address when trying to sketch evolutionary patterns in the current food system and its development in the foreseeable future.

*The food system is multidimensional and ranges from global to local, from farm to fork, from McDonald's to Michelin gourmet restaurants, from scientific laboratories to supermarket shelves*

Our focal points are threefold. In the first place we concentrate on market mechanisms. The chapters collected in this part of the book focus on the main drivers at work in the food system. The worldwide expansion of the food system into a global village is the underlying dimension of this part of the book, so to speak. For this reason, the consequences of globalisation are an issue of prime concern. Particular interest also goes to drivers which are relatively new to the evolving food system. In this respect, attention is devoted to such topics as foreign direct investments, and the impact of the biofuel boom on the world food market. The authors describe the food system's cutting edge developments in a way that reveals surprising mechanisms and unexpected outcomes.

In the second place this volume brings together a trio of varied chapters. By taking 'Software Becoming Hardware' as a heading, we collect several contributions showing that food production and consumption cannot be understood only in 'rational' terms of efficiency and economies of scale, nutritional value, price tags, product qualities, convenience or availability, but need also to be conceived as a matter of emotions, ethics as well as aesthetics.

A more clear and complete picture of today's and tomorrow's food world requires that we are not blind to the symbolic or moral values of food production and consumption. Taken together, the authors point to a group of factors that are supposed to be key: sustainability, transparency, corporate social responsibility, and safety. The underlying dimension in this part is the combination and confrontation of supply side phenomena and demand side tendencies at both poles of the food chain.

*Food production and consumption cannot be understood only in 'rational' terms of efficiency and economies of scale, nutritional value, price tags, product qualities, convenience or availability, but need also to be conceived as a matter of emotions, ethics as well as aesthetics*

In the third place we choose to dedicate some space in this book to issues and challenges which are of special interest to food policy and to the research agenda underlying food policymaking in the forthcoming years. In part 4 we flag up various issues for further research and bring several challenges for practical policymaking to the fore. In general, the conclusion is that there exists clearly a need for more research and reflection on a variety of questions in the field of both food studies and food policy. The underlying dimension in this part goes from practical issues and challenges that food policy is facing to additional theoretical questions that merits scholarly attention.

In the final chapter of this book we summarise the main lessons that can be learned from the preceding chapters. Our conclusions concentrate on issues and challenges which are not to be neglected with respect to anticipating the future of the global food system.

# Part 2

# Market structures, mechanisms and materials

# Globalisation in the food industry: the impact on market structures and firm postures

*Arjen van Witteloostuijn*

The academic literature and popular press argue that economic globalisation is gaining ground due to market liberalisation and technological progress. This chapter reflects on the likely impact of economic globalisation on the food industry. The emphasis is on the consequences for market structures and firm postures. Applying a resource-based theory of market structure and firm posture generates six propositions, predicting that, on average, economic globalisation in the food industry will increase both market concentration *and* density, due to worldwide consumer preference convergence *and* regional taste differentiation. As a result, the expectation is that large generalist food companies will grow *and* that the viability of small specialist food incumbents and newcomers will increase. Moreover, it is argued that the density rather than the concentration effect is likely to dominate.

## Two misunderstandings

Globalisation is a hotly debated issue, across the board and in the food industry (Friedman, 2006; Traill, 1997). Much of the debate is hindered by two misunderstandings (Brakman *et al.*, 2006). The first misunderstanding is the result of mixing different *types* of globalisation. For instance, cultural globalisation is different from institutional globalisation, and neither of the two directly involves economic globalisation. Cultural globalisation involves the widespread diffusion of Anglophone, particularly American, cultural products, from popular music to Hollywood movies, and to neo-liberal philosophies and star icons. The worldwide spread of neo-liberal philosophies has triggered a process of institutional globalisation, with the IMF, World Bank and WTO as the carriers of the gospel of market liberalisation. Both types of forces may well fuel economic globalisation, but not necessarily so. To make matters even more complicated, economic globalisation has different sides as well. For example, foreign direct investment (FDI) is related to international trade, but the relationship may go either way. That is, FDI and international trade can be complements, implying a positive link, or substitutes, producing a negative association. Moreover, demand-side globalisation may or may not work in tandem with supply-side globalisation. If both interact positively, for instance, global consumer taste convergence will trigger FDI and/ or international trade. These and many other subtleties imply that a discussion of the nature and impact of economic globalisation is not as straightforward as one might expect at first glance.

This chapter seeks to shed some light on a few key aspects of the debate, with an emphasis on what can be expected to happen in the realm of the food industry's market structures and firm postures. Let's be clear from the outset: we are referring to firm postures rather than firm strategies. There is much literature on firm strategies in the food industry dealing with a wide array of specific firm-level strategic issues, often referring to the 'optimal' way to produce value. In this chapter, the argument deals not so much with such specific strategic issues, but rather with a food firm's overall strategic posture in the marketplace.

The second misunderstanding emerges in the context of economic globalisation per se, relating to the *nature* and the *impact* of globalisation processes. In Main Street and in the popular press, many argue that the downsides of economic globalisation are dominant. There is much talk about the erosion of the 'competitive advantage' of nation-states, implying increasing unemployment and poverty in former islands of welfare such as the European Union and the United States. This argument is reflected in the rhetoric of many observers and politicians. Local businesses are said to move to low-wage countries, imports from emerging economies like China and India is argued to depress local production, and immigration is believed to produce a new underclass.

A much-read example is *The World is Flat*, published by the *New York Times* journalist Thomas Friedman in 2005. Presenting frightening anecdotes after terrifying statistics, he argues that Americans face frightful competition from Chinese rivals. Of course, globalisation, like any economic process, comes with its downsides. Particularly in the short run, some lose and some win. However, in the longer run, economic globalisation is a win-win scenario. This is the second misunderstanding: economic globalisation is about a country's comparative advantage – not competitive advantage. Arguing that nation-states benefit from competitive advantages or suffer from competitive disadvantages is economic nonsense. This fundamental insight was already forcefully put forward by the British 19<sup>th</sup> century economist David Ricardo, and is reflected in the modern view of the 2008 Nobel-prize winner Paul Krugman. This chapter deals with this Ricardian imagery of economic globalisation – nothing more, and nothing less.

*In the longer run, economic globalisation is a win-win scenario*

## Focus on economic globalisation

Economic globalisation triggers changes on both the demand and supply side in food markets. For instance, specific brands such as Coke and Mars are popular in Tokyo, Tehran, Rome, Lima and Los Angeles, and the Internet facilitates coordination of ICT activities in India, manufacturing in Poland, finance in the UK and design in Italy within a single firm. Of course, the food industry is facing other types of globalisation as well. For instance, it is argued that cultural globalisation in the food industry is increasing worldwide obesity (Popkin, 2006), and the global diffusion of genetically modified crop technology is said to contaminate nature (Belcher *et al.*, 2005). These types of globalisation are taken into account here to the extent that they affect the economics of globalisation. For example, globalisation may imply that particular food habits spread across the globe, triggering processes of worldwide preference convergence.

Fast food giant McDonald's is an oft-cited example. Hamburgers are now popular in New York, Paris, Moscow, Damascus, New Delhi, Djakarta, Sao Paolo, Mexico City, Lagos and Beijing, although the precise recipe is often subtly adapted to local taste and habit. We are not interested here in the cultural implications of this, but only in the economic effects – if there are any.

It is important to understand the likely impact of economic globalisation in the food industry, from agriculture and food processing to food retail and service. After all, the food industry is a large and critical part of any society: it is large, as it already amounted to more than four trillion US dollars sales worldwide in 2002 (Regmi and Gehlhar, 2005); it is critical, because it produces key nutrition for the population. All this became very apparent, again, in the food price crisis of 2007-2008. All countries need a food industry, and all countries have one, although market size is strongly related to a country's average per capita income. In this respect, the developing world is catching up, revealing much higher growth rates than the developed countries for more than a decade already. The dual question is how modern processes of economic globalisation impact upon this critical industry, and to what extent economic globalisation will facilitate or hinder this much-needed game of catch-up. This chapter reflects on this pair of issues.

*The developing world is catching up, revealing much higher growth rates than the developed countries for more than a decade already*

Note that this chapter's analysis is *ceteris paribus*, in two respects. First, as mentioned above, the focus is on the likely impact of economic globalisation. Second, the emphasis is on the meso-level of analysis of market structures and the micro-level of firm postures. In contrast to the majority of earlier studies, this study will only indirectly relate to macro-level issues by reflecting upon the critical role of meso-level market structures and micro-level firm postures in determining the vitality of macro-level communities such as countries and regions in the appraisal.

## Globalisation and market concentration in the food industry

The empirical and theoretical literature aimed at estimating the economic impact of globalisation in the food industry is generally rather positive about the economic consequences of globalisation (see e.g., Cioffi and dell'Aquila, 2004; Gow and Swinnen, 1998; Rae and Josling, 2003; Winters, 2005). Barriers to international investment and trade come in many different shapes and sizes, from straightforward import tariffs or export subsidies to subtle food safety and health-protecting regulation. To facilitate the favourable process of international specialisation, the autonomous processes of globalisation have to be stimulated by market liberalisation, per country and region (particularly the EU and the US), as well as worldwide (through the WTO). And indeed, this is what is happening, by and large (see, e.g. Trotter and Gordon, 2000).

*We still know little about the effect of globalisation on market structures and firm postures*

Of course, a major transition like this will be associated with losers, even when there are more winners. But even then, the argument goes, the long-run impact on welfare will be positive, for both the developed and the developing world. In the end, the underlying logic is exemplary and straightforward Ricardian international economics: with the free movement of capital and labour, countries will specialise according to the logic of comparative advantage. Large food companies will transmit such advantages by 'slicing up the value chain' on a global scale, whereas small food companies will benefit from locational advantages. This will imply an increase in both FDI and international trade. As a result, prices will be lower, and innovations will be stimulated. This increases consumer surplus across the board. The literature gives rise to another observation, though: we still know little about the effect of globalisation on issues at lower levels of analyses, particularly market structures and firm postures (for some reflections on these issues, see Traill, 1997). Exploring this pair of issues in greater detail is the focus of the remainder of this chapter.

Work by Chris Boling and Mark Gehlhar (2005) is interesting as it concerns empirical information on market structures and firm postures. Overall, the largest food companies account for less than 3% of worldwide food sales – not very impressive, to put it mildly. Although, on average, market concentration is low in the food industry, it can be much higher for specific markets, particularly in the processed food segment, which tends to feature larger scale and scope economies, as well as more consumer taste convergence. Table 1 provides illustrative figures for the concentration ratios ($C_1$ to $C_6$) for the six largest food companies in the world – Nestlé, Kraft, Unilever, PepsiCo, Danone and Mars – in twenty processed food markets.

For instance, market concentration is relatively high in the ice cream (with a $C_4$ of 30.3%), savory snacks (36.0) and dog and cat food (50.2) markets. However, in 13 out of 20 processed food markets, the $C_4$ is below 20%. As far as firm postures are concerned, only one large food company – Nestlé – spans across all twenty processed food categories, with Kraft (19) and Unilever (17) following closely behind. Among the Big Six, PepsiCo (9), Danone (9) and Mars (10) are, relatively speaking, specialist rather than generalist food companies. This observation is backed by the fact that half of the Big Six have small market shares in their leading market – Kraft with 5.7% in ready meals, Danone with 4.8% in dairy products, and Mars with 9.4% in confectionery. In most non-processed food markets, these figures are likely to be (much) lower.

## Typologies and activities

Before we turn to an analysis of economic globalisation on market structures and firm postures in the food industry, it is useful to first clarify what this type of globalisation may be about. The first manifestation of economic globalisation is international trade. This is not new, of course. Already before World War I, the global economy reached a peak in the volume and value of international trade (Bordo *et al.*, 2003). A second manifestation of economic globalisation is FDI (see the Chapter by Bunte in this volume).

Table 1. Concentration in the Food Industry in 2002 (Euromonitor, 2003).

| Product category | $C_1$ | $C_2$ | $C_3$ | $C_4$ | $C_5$ | $C_6$ |
|---|---|---|---|---|---|---|
| Confectionery | 9.4 | 18.4 | 24.0 | - | - | - |
| Bakery products | 3.0 | 4.7 | 5.9 | 6.9 | 7.4 | - |
| Ice cream | 19.3 | 28.2 | 30.1 | 30.3 | 30.4 | - |
| Dairy products | 4.8 | 9.2 | 12.9 | 13.2 | - | - |
| Savory snacks | 32.4 | 35.4 | 35.7 | 36.0 | 36.0 | - |
| Snack bars | 9.9 | 15.6 | 19.7 | 22.8 | 24.5 | 25.8 |
| Meal replacement drinks | 38.7 | 38.9 | - | - | - | - |
| Ready meal | 9.7 | 15.4 | 18.4 | 19.2 | 19.4 | - |
| Soup | 17.3 | 24.2 | 24.2 | - | - | - |
| Pasta | 4.6 | 7.7 | 8.1 | 8.5 | - | - |
| Noodles | 1.3 | 2.6 | 3.0 | - | - | - |
| Canned food | 1.1 | 1.8 | 2.4 | 2.8 | - | - |
| Frozen food | 6.1 | 10.3 | 12.7 | - | - | - |
| Dried food | 3.3 | 6.5 | 8.8 | 9.6 | 9.8 | - |
| Chilled food | 2.6 | 3.5 | 3.7 | - | - | - |
| Oils and fats | 13.4 | 14.0 | 14.4 | 14.7 | - | - |
| Sauces, dressings and condiments | 10.7 | 15.0 | 18.0 | 18.8 | 19.5 | 20.2 |
| Baby food | 16.9 | 18.5 | 18.7 | 18.9 | 19.0 | - |
| Spreads | 7.1 | 9.3 | 9.9 | 10.2 | 10.4 | - |
| Dog and cat food | 25.7 | 49.7 | 50.2 | - | - | - |

Notes: own calculations on the basis of the global sales share of the top six (Nestlé, Kraft, Unilever, PepsiCo, Danone and Mars), where - indicates that the lower-ranked top-six companies have zero sales. Of course, the actual degree of market concentration may well be higher, if other food companies than the overall top six are leading in specific markets. $C_1$ denotes the market share of the largest firm in the industry, $C_2$ denotes the market share of the two largest firms in the industry, etc.

A popular foreign entry mode is through merger and acquisition activities, next to alliance formation and greenfield investment (Dikova and Van Witteloostuijn, 2008). Much of this involves 'slicing up the value chain' (Krugman, 1995), implying insourcing and outsourcing at the country level. The argument, in a nutshell, runs as follows. As a result of new technologies (particularly in the area of information and communication) and new opportunities (particularly market liberalisation, including the rise of emerging and transition economies), modern companies can look for lower costs and higher profits by locating and relocating activities to those places where costs are low or markets are growing. This reflects efficiency-seeking and market-seeking FDI, respectively.

*It is not so much industries as a whole that are on the move, but rather activities that may cross multiple industries*

Modern processes of economic globalisation imply that the standard industry classification is now largely obsolete, if we want to study the effect that these modern globalisation processes might have on the local economy. Instead, for this purpose, we must focus on activities that cross traditional industry boundaries. This is no different in the food industry. To illustrate this observation, it is useful to discuss briefly an instance of 'traditional' globalisation *vis-à-vis* a modern process of globalisation. On the one hand, a traditional example of globalisation relates to the textile industry, which was largely relocated as an industry. This implies that, due to shifts in comparative advantages, whole industries move from one part of the world to the other. Being a labour-intensive industry, textile moved primarily from the rich West to low-wage countries in the East. On the other hand, a modern example of the likely impact of globalisation involves radiology activities. Now, it is not so much industries as a whole that are on the move, but rather activities that may cross multiple industries. This type of international mobility is facilitated by modern information and communication technologies. Radiology reports (or any other information that can be transmitted via the Internet) can be transferred from one side of the globe to the other in a split second.

## Substitutability and transferability

How economic globalisation will work out at the activity level very much depends upon the relative strength of two forces, which both tend to be activity and/or country (or region) specific.

The first force is the extent of substitutability of activities. This force is not so much driven by globalisation processes per se, but rather by a combination of shifts in societal demand patterns and changes in technological opportunities. If specific needs can be satisfied in a variety of ways, substitutability is an issue. With technological progress, substitutability may kill activities or industries. The automobile made horse carriages obsolete, by and large. With shifts in preferences, one activity or industry may push aside another. Demand for computer games harms the music industry.

The second force is the extent of transferability of activities. Only if activities are transferable, can relocation effects emerge. Due to decreased transportations costs and increased technological opportunities more activities than ever are transferable. The radiology example above is illustrative. But take the counterexample of a barber. In principle, this is a low-cost activity. For someone living in Paris or New York, attending a barber in Beijing, however cheap, is not an option. This activity is location-bound. Combining both forces in matrix form, for the sake of simplicity, produces the classification of four ideal-typical cases reproduced in Table 2.

*Table 2. A classification of four ideal-typical cases.*

|  | Substitutable activities | Non-substitutable activities |
| --- | --- | --- |
| Non-transferable activities | Inter-industry drift | Industry status quo |
| Transferable activities | International specialisation | Sourcing flow |

In the ideal-typical case of *Industry status quo*, nothing changes if the activities are non-substitutable and non-transferable. Local food retailing is local by definition, both in terms of the nature of the activity and the physical location of this activity. The same is true for local specialities tailored at local tastes, such as region-specific liquor.

In the case of *Inter-industry drift*, shifts within or across industries are local if activities are non-transferable but substitutable. An example is bio-fuel production, which is increasing exponentially in the EU, the US and elsewhere. This comes at the expense of the local production of agricultural products for food purposes. As a result, food prices will go up.

Within the context of *Sourcing flow*, activities that are non-substitutable but transferable move to the location that offers comparative advantage. For instance, the production of labour-intensive and tradeable food such as sugar would, in the absence of artificial trade barriers, relocate to low-cost countries, particularly in the developing world.

Finally, with respect to *International specialisation*, some activities are both substitutable and transferable. A case in point is artificial sweeteners, which can replace natural sugar. Then, some countries develop a comparative advantage in the substitute activity, which often happens to be in the developed world. In parallel, much remaining food production (natural sugar, in the example) is shifting to developing countries.

The above examples all involve industries or products. In the modern globalised world, slicing up the value chain implies that specific horizontal or vertical activities are separated, and relocated to the spot offering a comparative advantage. For instance, large food-processing multinational enterprises (MNEs) such as Proctor & Gamble and Unilever may source raw food material in Brazil, perform ICT support in India, invest in R&D in Switzerland, and design ad campaigns in Britain. In this chapter, though, the focus is on the industry or product level.

## A theory of market structure and firm posture

From the above, we have learned that activities might potentially move to other countries or locations (transferability) and/or activities or industries (substitutability). Shifts in activities influence not only the international division of economic activities, but also market structures and firm postures. Recently, we (Van Witteloostuijn and Boone, 2006) suggested a so-called resource-based theory of market structure and firm posture. In this theory, insights from industrial organisation (IO) economics and organisational ecology (OE) sociology are combined to explain and predict what types of market structures and firm postures are likely to emerge under particular circumstances. Here, before applying their logic to the food industry, this theory is briefly introduced and focused on four building blocks: two antecedents (supply and demand conditions) and two consequences (market structures and firm postures).

The first antecedent condition relates to the supply side, in particular costs. Costs are reflected in economies of scale and scope. Scale economies imply lower average costs if more of a single product is produced by one and the same organisation. Scope economies imply lower average costs if a range of product varieties is produced by one company rather than more than one. This chapter focuses, for the sake of the argument, both polar cases with high *vis-à-vis* low economies of scale and scope.

The second antecedent condition relates to the demand side. Demand is determined by what is referred to as richness and evenness in biology. Richness is simply the number of varieties or niches in the industry: a larger number implies a richer resource base. Evenness has to do with the distribution of demand over these varieties. With high evenness and high richness, demand is equally distributed across a large number of product varieties. With high evenness and low richness, demand is concentrated in a limited number of niches. With low evenness and high richness, we have high demand in a limited number of niches and low demand in a large number of niches.

The first consequence of both antecedent conditions is manifest in market structures. In particular, the argument is that both demand and supply-side features map onto the market's concentration and density. Concentration refers to the degree of dominance of the larger players, and density to the mere number of organisations. Again, for the sake of the argument, the focus here is on high-low dichotomies. The four ideal type cases are summarised in Table 3 (for more details, the interested reader is referred to van Witteloostuijn and Boone, 2006).

First, with high concentration and high density, the market features a small number of large and a large number of small organisations, or a dual market structure. This outcome emerges when there is high demand for a small number of varieties and low demand for a large number of niche products. In the centre, large firms can benefit from scale economies; in the periphery, specialist producers offer tailor-made varieties without any scope economies. In IO terminology, this is a fringed oligopoly. A case in point is the beer industry (see below).

Second, with high concentration and low density, a small number of large single-variety producers dominate the market. This concentrated market structure is obtained, when for example consumers are not that interested in variety and there are scale economies on the supply side. This is the classic pure oligopoly case in IO. Natural sugar may be a case in point. Even when consumers are interested in variety, a few large multi-product multinational enterprises may

*Table 3. Classification of market structures.*

|                     | High density                              | Low density                                 |
|---------------------|-------------------------------------------|---------------------------------------------|
| High concentration  | Dual market structure (fringed oligopoly) | Concentrated market structure (pure oligopoly) |
| Low concentration   | Fragmented market structure (perfect competition) | Uniform market structure (monopolistic competition) |

very well dominate the marketplace. If there are economies of scope, multiproduct firms have an advantage over single product firms. One example may be the ice cream market.

Third, with low concentration and high density, the market structure is fragmented. For instance this structure features demand for a homogeneous product without any economies of scale and scope. In IO, the key example is perfect competition, with a large number of small enterprises. A case in point is agriculture.

Fourth, a market structure with low concentration and low density is referred to as uniform. Then, not so many and not so large firms operate in a market with demand equally distributed over a number of different varieties. Economies of scope are limited. In IO, a well-known example is monopolistic competition. Examples may the bread and confectionery markets.

The second consequence of both antecedent conditions is manifest in firm postures. Within a specific market structure, some firms do well, and others do not. This relates to firm postures, and to which firm postures perform viably in which market structure. Two choices are crucial: (1) whether the company targets a broad or a narrow niche, and (2) whether the organisation produces a single product or multiple products (or, to be precise, product varieties). Narrow-niche firms are called specialists, and their broad-niche counterparts are referred to as generalists. Combining both dimensions gives the four intuitive ideal types of firm postures summarised in Table 4. Take two examples of opposite firm postures from the beer industry, by way of

*Table 4. Classification of firm postures.*

|  | Single product | Multiple products |
|---|---|---|
| Narrow niche | Single-product specialist | Multi-product specialist |
| Broad niche | Single-product generalist | Multi-product generalist |

illustration: Dutch Heineken is a multi-product generalist operating globally, and Onder den Linden is a single-product specialist in the Dutch province of Limburg.

## Propositions for future research – 1

The above framework offers a platform for analysing the likely impact of processes of globalisation on the structure of food industries and the viability of food enterprises. The question is how globalisation processes, in conjunction and in interaction with other forces such as market liberalisation and technological progress, affect the demand side's resource space and the supply side's cost structure in the food industry. To answer this question, detailed and fine-grained information is needed for different markets and segments of the food industry, taking account of potential national or regional differences. An analysis like this would be beyond the scope of the current chapter. Instead, the focus here is on speculating about likely trends, as well as on providing a few examples. In this context, the propositions developed below might offer interesting benchmark predictions.

For one, the development of cost structures is heavily influenced by technological progress. Basically, as explained in the sustainability analysis of William Baumol, John Panzar and Robert Willig (1982), the key is to analyse potential shifts in typical single and multi-product cost curves. Here, only two benchmark arguments are offered. One, globalisation offers ample opportunities to increase the scale of production by producing standardised products for world markets – or, alternatively, a number of large regional markets. With improved transportation technologies and decreased regulatory trade barriers, and hence reduced transport cost, this strategy becomes more attractive, on average. Two, technological progress reduces the cost of multi-product production. For instance, modern ICT offers ample opportunities to share common resources more cheaply. An example is marketing, where similar e-communication techniques can be applied across a wide range of different products. So, the *first proposition* is that globalisation will increase the opportunities to reap scale and scope economies.

However, scale and scope economies are not isolated supply-side phenomena. For example, scale economies can only be reaped in those food markets that feature standardisation of production processes, worldwide (or large regional) demand for relatively homogeneous products, and opportunities to ship these products across space. Economies of scale and scope, then, will only materialise in markets where the demand side fits well with either type of economies. This is linked to the issue of shifts in the demand side's resource shape.

*In some food markets, worldwide demand convergence is the rule; in other food markets, local divergence is becoming more and more important*

The resource shapes in the food industry are said to change in two ways. That is, the literature on the development of demand for food emphasises two seemingly opposite developments: global convergence and regional differentiation. On the one hand, in some food markets, worldwide demand convergence is the rule. This is what may be called the McDonaldisation of food preferences. On the other hand, in other food markets, local divergence is becoming more and more important. Demand for differentiation is further enhanced by modern considerations of health and safety, as well as consumer worries about the environment. The consequence of all this is an increasing 'love for variety' (Feenstra, 2004). In many domains of the food industry, this trend is associated with much product innovation activity. In beverages, for instance, many new products were launched in the 1990s (e.g. isotonics and wellness juice) and 2000s (e.g. fortified waters and drinkable yoghurts). All this brings us to the *second proposition*: globalisation will increase taste convergence and love for variety, implying a larger peak and expanded peripheries.

## Propositions for future research – 2

Globalisation processes and technological innovations operate in tandem. On the one hand, globalisation could not have taken its current form and shape without modern information and communication technologies. On the other hand, without the large investment by the leading food companies in product innovations and marketing campaigns, the convergence of consumer preferences would have been less prominent. For the sake of brevity, we simply refer to globalisation as a shortcut reference to this tandem. Having said this, globalisation is likely to produce a few *trend* effects in the food industry. That is, overall, the food industry is expected to reveal a number of general trends. The first one is that, due to the average convergence of consumer taste, market concentration will probably increase. Thus, the *third proposition* reads as follows: globalisation (a) will increase market concentration in the food industry, from which (b) a subset of the generalist food companies across the value chain will benefit.

The large food companies in the world all seek growth. This is true for Nestlé, the globe's number one, as well as for rivals like Danone, Kraft and Unilever. In 1998-2002, Nestlé grew by an impressive 24.3%, and Unilever by a substantial but slightly less impressive 19.4%. Here, too, it is clear that the main growth markets can be found in the developing world, with Europe being the major laggard. Moreover, growth tends to be achieved by acquisitions: it is externally rather than internally driven. Much FDI by the globe's leading food companies takes this acquisition form. Take the example of Unilever. Unilever's impressive growth in North America is the result of acquiring large local companies such as Ben and Jerry's, and Slim Fast. The portfolio of the world's leading food companies is wide-ranging, both along the geographical and the product dimension. As of 2003, Nestlé was active in 20 product categories in about 150 countries, Unilever in 16 product categories in approximately 120 countries, and Danone in 16 product categories in 70 or so countries (Euromonitor, 2003).

However, increasing market concentration can be associated with either decreasing or increasing firm density. This leads to the second hypothesised trend effect. Apart from taste convergence, local differentiation is key. Actually, in quite a few national food industries, globalisation triggers a countermovement, in which domestic produce is cherished (Sorge, 2005). An example is the large number of local cheeses that are produced by domestic niche specialists in many countries across the world. In the Netherlands, for instance, worldwide cheese brands such as Edam and Gouda are produced next to a wide variety of local farm cheeses. These deliberations bring us to the *fourth proposition* about market density: globalisation (a) will increase market density in the food industry, from which (b) a subset of incumbent and many newcomer specialist food firms across the value chain will benefit.

Indeed, notwithstanding the growth of the world's leading food companies, the food industry is *not* dominated by them – quite to the contrary. This is immediately clear from the data in Table 1. However large the prominent food MNEs might be, and however impressive their growth rates may look like, they still are unable to really dominate the global food industry. Overall, after all, the summed market shares of the world's leading food companies are low. This suggests a *fifth proposition*: (a) the density effect will be stronger than the concentration effect, implying that (b) particularly specialist viability in the food industry will increase in the slipstream of globalisation.

So, high concentration (globalisation) and high density (regionalisation) may well co-evolve in parallel. The result is the emergence or further proliferation of dual market structures, with generalists and specialists viably operating side by side. Some products are locally produced and consumed, others locally produced and globally consumed, and yet others globally produced and globally consumed. This paradox is reflected in the *sixth* 'glocalisation' *proposition*: globalisation will trigger regionalisation, and regionalisation will boost globalisation.

Of course, exceptions will confirm the above rules. That is, in specific sub-markets of the food industry, defined along geographical and product lines, deviation effects are likely to turn out to be dominant. In some markets, the fundamental characteristics on the demand and supply side (i.e. resource shapes and exploitation economies) are such that the impact of globalisation may be either neutral or different, or similar but less forceful. Salt or sugar markets are two cases in point (Sutton, 1991). Because there is little demand for product differentiation, by far the majority of the consumers - perceiving salt as salt and sugar as sugar - are interested in price alone. So, in these food markets, one may expect shifts – if there are any – that are less impressive than in many other sectors of the food industry, such as beer. But still, the tendency may be similar to the one reflected in the six propositions.

## Glocalisation in the beer industry

A nice example of a food market in which all six propositions find support is the beer brewing industry, as reported by Glenn Carroll and Anand Swaminathan (2000). Indeed, there is a striking contrast between the density evolution of generalist mass producers vis-à-vis that of their specialist counterparts. The number of mass producers dropped from 641 in 1938 to 22 in 1997 (Figure 1). This came with a massive increase of market concentration, from a $C_4$ of 13.5% in 1938 to 90.2 in 1997. Notwithstanding the increasing dominance of the large generalist beer breweries, new small specialist breweries started to emerge in the late 1970s in the form of microbreweries, initially, and brewpubs (and to much more limited extent, contract brewers) later. In 1975, the number of specialist breweries was one, the density of mass producers was 53 and the $C_4$ was 58.4: the US beer brewing industry seemed clearly on its way to an oligopoly structure, dominated by a small number of large generalists. In 1997, the density of specialist brewers had increased to a temporary peak of 1,334. In the 1990s, an era of accelerating economic globalisation, the $C_4$ increased from 87.6 in 1990 to 90.2 in 1997, the number of mass producers declined slightly from 23 in 1990 to 22 in 1997, and the density of small specialists breweries increased from 564 in 1990 to 1,334 in 1997. This is a classic example of resource partitioning, which was further stimulated in the recent period of economic globalisation, offering an illustration of the third, fourth and fifth proposition.

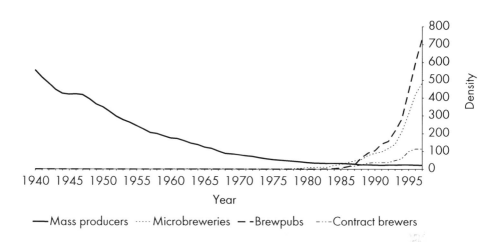

Figure 1. Density evolution in the US beer brewing industry in 1938-1997.

## Future work on the challenges of globalisation

Current globalisation implies that precisely the combination of a need for variety, scale economies in mass markets, and lack of scope economies in market fringes is likely to dominate in many food markets of the future, as illustrated by the beer industry example. In terms of firm postures, this chapter's analysis suggests that two types of posture are likely to do particularly well in the years to come: large-firm multi-domestic generalist postures and small-firm local specialist postures. This logic implies that globalisation is a *trigger* of localisation. Precisely because large global generalists grow larger, niches emerge in which local specialists can flourish. The hypothesis, then, is that the latter density-increasing effect will be stronger than the former concentration-increasing effect. Future work is needed to collect evidence that might support or undermine this theory.

*The combination of a need for variety, scale economies in mass markets, and lack of scope economies in market fringes is likely to dominate in many food markets of the future*

Globalisation is a challenge, for sure. This is not only true for research, but also for policy (Pinstrup-Andersen, 2000). From this perspective, it is even more important in future work to link the above-sketched analysis to two key challenges that face the world in general and the global food industry in particular. First, the current environmental and climate crisis is, at least in part, due to the negative externalities of economic activities, including food production (see also Henning Steinfeld's chapter in this book). Specifically, food production may be associated with environmental damage, such as the destruction of the natural habitat of species and the discharge of $CO_2$. In this context, many argue that much food is currently improperly priced, not taking account of such negative externalities. Second, poverty is still a key issue in developing countries. In such countries, agriculture and food production are crucial. Hence, a critical condition for global poverty reduction are Western markets that are open to food imports from the developing world, as well as tailor-made protection and stimulation of local agriculture and food industries outside the West. An intriguing question is how different market structures may contribute differently to environmental damage and poverty reduction.

# The food economy of today and tomorrow

*Frank Bunte*

In the first decades of the post-World War II period, the food economy was simple. There was little food supply for a deserving population. Food shortage was not only due to the destructions caused by the war, but also to the way agricultural production was organised: i.e. small scale and highly dependent on low-skilled, manual labour. Food policy, consequently, was directed at promoting food supply as well as restructuring farm organisation. The geographical scope of the food economy was limited to OECD countries, because the socialist economies were not integrated into the world economy and production in developing countries, with some exceptions, was dominated by subsistence farming. Moreover, agricultural and food markets were highly protected. In those days, food companies had a relatively easy job with demand exceeding supply and international competition excluded.

Recently, the deserving populations of OECD countries – and in fact many developing countries – have turned obese due to excess supply of subsidised food production. Food markets in OECD countries are highly saturated which makes consumers very demanding in terms of convenience, variety and quality. Moreover, consumers and other stakeholders, notably NGOs, increasingly stress the importance of such ethical aspects of food production and consumption as food safety, animal welfare, fairness and the environment. The geographical scope of the food economy has become global with trade barriers disappearing, the former socialist countries integrating into the world economy and developing countries bridging the productivity and income gaps with OECD countries. In this context, food companies and governments are trying to redefine their strategies and policies.

## Changes and challenges

Food companies face the challenge of meeting the increasing demands of consumers on the one hand, while controlling costs and prices and upholding a solid bottom line on the other. At the same time, food companies are increasingly addressing social responsibilities by developing CSR schemes and private standards. Governments study whether they have to define policies for such new emerging social issues as obesity, food safety and animal welfare. Besides the fact that governments want to develop policies with respect to new issues, they face two administrative problems. How to guarantee policy coherence when the number of policy areas and objectives is proliferating? How to match public responsibilities with private ones?

In this chapter, we discuss some of the more major changes in the food economy as well as the challenges food companies have to address. The focus is on four changes in the global food economy which affect consumer demand and international economic relations and have implications for food company strategies. The first of the four changes we concentrate on concerns differences in population and income growth in the global food economy, that is, the share of developing countries in global food demand, supply and trade grows, while the share of developed countries falls. The second deals with the growing demand for convenience, variety and quality. In developing countries, food demand is shifting from rice and cereals to meat, dairy, fruits and vegetables. In developed as well as developing countries, food demand is shifting from home to out-of-home consumption and from fresh commodities to prepared food. Consumers eat an ever wider variety of food at ever higher quality levels. As a result of this development, trade in value-added products is increasing. Food companies are individualising food supply and increasingly deliver at home. The third trend emphasised in this chapter is about the world becoming one market place. Even though there remain important regional differences in food demand, cultural globalisation leads to a convergence of consumer taste as well as distribution patterns. With trade barriers falling, the food economy is turning into a single market place. This opens up production and trade opportunities for both developed and developing countries. The opening up of markets is an opportunity for individual companies, even though the business environment is becoming more competitive. The fourth development discussed in this chapter highlights the fact that sustainability issues give rise to ethical considerations throughout the food economy. Consumers and other stakeholders such as NGOs require socially responsible products. Consumers increasingly buy ethical food. In the trade context, New Trade Concerns emerge in order to take account of ethical considerations. Companies take up the sustainability challenge by implementing CSR schemes and applying private standards.

## The rise of the developing world

One of the main characteristics of the current globalisation process is the fact that the world is increasingly extending beyond North America, Western and Southern Europe, Japan, Australia and New Zealand. Russia, Central Europe and China have opened up their economies and to some extent their societies in the last two decades and have become major players in the world economy. Economic growth is taking place in the developing world. By 2020, the population in developing countries will have grown by more than 20% (UN, 2007), while per capita income in developing countries will have doubled (LEI, 2009). Driven by rapid population and income growth, the share of developing countries in the world economy will rise rapidly, while the share of OECD countries, notably Europe and Japan, will fall.

Population and income growth are leading to an enormous rise in the demand for food. The growth in per capita income will cause a major change in the diet of third world countries. There is a major shift from cereals and rice to meat, dairy, fats and oils, fruit and vegetables (Figure 1). Because there is a surge in the demand for food, food prices are under pressure. Food prices are under further pressure, because an increasing part of crop production is used for the production of bio-fuels (see the following chapter in this volume). Dairy and meat production are particularly demanding, because

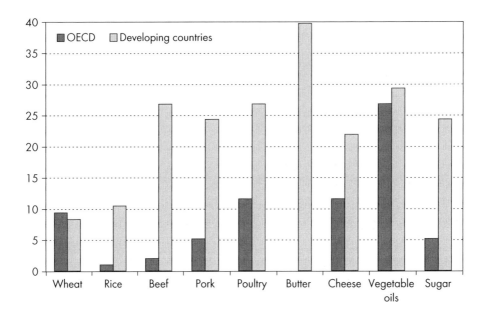

*Figure 1. Consumption of food in OECD and developing countries: 2007-2016 (% Change) (OECD-FAO, 2007).*

they require coarse grains and oilseeds and thus vast amounts of land. Most projections confidently show that supply will be able to meet demand and soften the pressure on prices in the next decade (LEI, 2009; OECD, 2007). Farmers may increase crop yields by intensifying the use of fertilisers. Policy restrictions on supply – for instance, milk quota – may be relaxed.

*Agricultural exports will grow in developing rather than developed countries in the coming decade*

The share of the developing world is also growing on the supply side. As a result of a rise in the workforce, the area of land used for agricultural production (South America) and factor productivity, developing countries are able to boost their production and exports. As a result, agricultural exports will grow in developing rather than developed countries in the coming decade (Figure 2). The gap between developed and developing countries in terms of factor productivity will gradually diminish. Some people expect that physical product characteristics will increasingly be commoditized

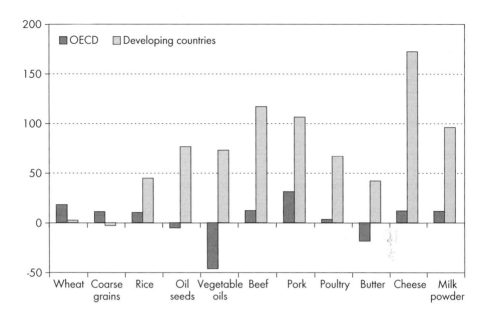

*Figure 2. Exports of food from OECD and developing countries: 2007-2016 (% Change) (OECD-FAO, 2007).*

(Jacobs, 2007). As a result, OECD countries may well lose their comparative advantage in the production of high-quality food products to developing countries such as Brazil, Thailand and China. If so, the European, American or Japanese part of the supply chain may very well be restricted to the services attached to the production of food products, such as marketing, R&D and retail distribution. Developing countries are starting to resemble developed countries. Food companies in developing countries are beginning to act like their counterparts in developed countries.

One should bear in mind that important differences exist in the economic development of developing countries. Contrary to countries like China, India and Brazil, economic development in the least developed countries is likely to remain poor in the coming decade. Due to, for example, unfavourable soil and climate conditions, many of the least developed countries remain net importers of food. For most agricultural commodities, their share in world exports will be far less than 1% in 2016. There are also important differences in the role that agriculture and food play in economic development. In Latin American countries such as Brazil, agricultural production and trade are among the main drivers of economic growth. In China, manufacturing rather than agriculture is the main driver of economic growth. The rise in the Chinese standard of living is reflected in higher food consumption and higher food imports. Chinese net import demand for cereals, coarse grains and other food items will probably continue to put upward pressure on food prices in the decades to come.

## Convenience, variety and quality

Changes in per capita income and demographics also influence the demand for food qualitatively. In OECD countries food markets are saturated, because consumers are well off. Consumers spend additional income on such services as health care and tourism rather than food. However, when buying food, consumers also spend more on convenience and service. Food service is growing rapidly all over the world. In developed countries, retail sales of prepared food – such as ready-to-eat meals – are growing increasingly fast (5-7% annually). The rapid growth of prepared food in developed countries is facilitated further by the wide availability of household amenities such as microwaves and refrigerators.

With income rising, consumption patterns are becoming more varied at both macro and micro levels. In a high income country such as the USA, the top 5 product categories account for 48% of food sales. In a lower income country such as Mexico, the top 5 product categories account for 71% of food sales. Within product categories, variety is also increasing (see Knowles, 2007). In the 1970s, consumers basically drank coffee, tea, milk, juice and soft drinks. In the 1980s, the product assortment was widened with bottled waters and RTD teas and juices. In the 1990s, wellness juices and teas, isotonics, RTD coffees and flavoured teas were added. In the 2000s, soy beverages, functional beverages, fortified waters, drinkable yogurts and hybrid products followed.

The increase in the demand for convenience, quality and variety is reflected in international trade. Trade in agriculture and food is shifting from raw produce to value added products such as fresh produce (fruit, vegetables) and manufactured products. Following ERS (2005), one can make a distinction between commodity-based products and manufactured products. The former are identifiable with one agricultural input, such as milk, meat or sugar. Manufactured products undergo substantial transformation and cannot be identified with one principal agricultural input (bakery products, confectionery, baby food). Table 1 shows that trade in manufactured products is growing faster than trade in commodity-based products. The share of manufactured food and beverages in OECD food trade increased from 25% in 1993 to 30% in 2004.

*Trade in manufactured products is growing faster than trade in commodity-based products*

For food companies, the demand for convenience, quality and variety is a major challenge. Suppliers need to deliver whatever food consumers want, wherever and whenever they want it. The demand for convenience is likely to cause major revolutions in food distribution. Consumers will choose those distribution channels which reduce their shopping time as well as food preparation time.

*Table 1. OECD food exports in 2004 (WTO).*

| Product group | Exports (USD billion) | Annual growth 1993-2004 |
| --- | --- | --- |
| Raw materials (e.g. meat) | 74.5 | 3.1 |
| Fresh commodities (e.g. fruit) | 82.7 | 5.6 |
| Processed products | 142.4 | 5.6 |
|     Commodity-based products (e.g. dairy) | 83.7 | 4.7 |
|     Manufactured products (e.g. flavourings) | 58.7 | 7.0 |
| Beverages | 46.2 | 7.3 |
| Total | 345.8 | 5.2 |

For this reason, internet sales, home deliveries and convenience stores are likely to grow. The last mile will be one of the main competition arenas in food retail in the next decade. Internet sales and home deliveries are expected to become important for repeat purchases of such everyday necessities as milk, soft drinks, potatoes and apples (Jacobs, 2007). Future retail outlets will combine the delivery of an increasingly wider product assortment that will include ethical drugs, postal services and social services (e.g. home meals). These developments will have major consequences for food logistics as well as for store and format design. When designing the future retail outlet, one should take into account that both home-delivered products and intermediary products such as fats and oils will become less prominently available relative to ready-to-eat meals. Home delivery implies that logistics go one step further, which may require a reorganisation of retail distribution. Home delivery also has consequences for congestion, especially in urban areas, as well as greenhouse gas emissions. Home deliveries may seem harmful in terms of $CO_2$ emissions and congestion, but one should bear in mind that the current organisation of the last mile – i.e. everyone taking their own car – does not perform very well in this respect either.

*The last mile will be one of the main competition arenas in food retail in the next decade*

## Networking

Food companies will enter into a dialogue with consumers in order to find out what they want. Information technology will play a key role in this 'consumer networking'. Food companies will increasingly use information technologies to send generic or specific offers to consumers and to receive responses and demands from consumers. Consumers will share their personal information (address, health, payment cards, loyalty programmes) with the supply chain, provided the chain is able to create and maintain trust among consumers that the privacy of this information will be safeguarded. In the next ten years, the food supply chain will invest heavily in information technology and data analysis in order to get and keep in touch with the consumer.

The food supply chain will also individualise food supply in order to meet the demand for variety. The era of mass production is over. Mass production may remain important for the production of food ingredients, but it will become less important for end products. Product batches will become ever smaller. Because product quality and variety are becoming more important and individualised, product research and development is becoming riskier than ever. For this reason, food companies may be expected to consult consumers during the R&D process. Indeed, companies such as Lego and Procter & Gamble already involve consumers in R&D processes. Moreover, supply chain co-ordination with respect to product development is also expected to increase the efficiency and lower the risks involved.

*Firms that cooperate are more likely to innovate and do so successfully, than firms that do not cooperate*

SMEs may be expected to benefit from the demand for quality and variety, since they are better equipped than large corporations to offer gourmet innovations (see the previous chapter in this volume). There are two factors which have a decisive impact on the ability of SMEs to innovate. Firstly, a minimum scale is necessary in order to innovate. Larger SMEs are more likely to innovate than smaller SMEs. On the other hand, size may matter only for R&D-related innovations. In this remark it is noteworthy that the innovation literature concentrates on R&D but 'often fails to capture changes in design or materials that significantly modify products but do not result in the creation of an entirely new product' (Vindigni *et al.*, 2006: 123). Secondly, participation in networks enhances innovation activities. Firms that cooperate with competitors, suppliers, customers and research institutes are more likely to innovate and do so successfully than firms that do not cooperate. 'The key problem for small firms appears not to be that of being small, but of being isolated' (Pyke *et al.*, 1990: 4). The major disadvantage SMEs have *vis-à-vis* corporate enterprise is the fact that SMEs have limited resources. SMEs do not have specialised resources at their disposal, at least not all kinds of resources. Thus, it is important that SMEs embed their firms in networks where such required resources are available.

## The world as one market place

For at least three reasons, the world is turning into one market place. Firstly, time and distance shrink as travel and transportation time and costs continue to fall rapidly. Secondly, due to advances in information technology, news is available worldwide within seconds. Thirdly, the economic liberalisation of sectors (agriculture and food, but also transport and telecommunication) and entire economies (China and Russia) connects formerly protected markets to the world economy.

As a consequence of these processes, there is rapid convergence in consumption patterns. Multinationals are present worldwide, partly because consumers all want to go to McDonald's to drink Coca Cola and eat French fries. Western brands and multinationals are becoming established in developing countries. Food distribution in middle income developing countries is increasingly organised in the same way as it is in Western countries. Supermarkets of domestic and Western origin are rapidly becoming the most prominent distribution channel for food. In Brazil, for instance, supermarkets increased their market share in food retail from 30 to 75% in the 1990s. In Western countries, this process took half a century.

*Food distribution in middle income developing countries is increasingly organised in the same way as it is in Western countries*

Nevertheless, there remain important regional differences in the demand for food, among other things due to differences in income and cultural preferences. Fish consumption is more prevalent in Asian countries than in Europe and North America, while the opposite holds for dairy. In northern Europe and the USA, beer is more popular than wine, while the opposite applies in the Mediterranean region. There remain large cultural differences in the way people have breakfast, lunch or dinner. In fact, the product assortment of a multinational food service company such as McDonald's differs from one country to the other. In Germany, McDonald's serves sauerkraut and in Portugal customers can order soup at the restaurants of McDonald's. Finally, there are major differences in the quantities and packaging of food items sold in supermarkets: quantities and packaging are customised to local habits and preferences.

With respect to international trade, one may expect further liberalisation of agricultural and food markets in the next decade. Current proposals at the Doha round imply major reductions in tariffs on agricultural commodities and food. Moreover, there is a proliferation of bilateral and regional trade and investment agreements. Agriculture and food remain one of the world's most heavily protected markets. Before the Uruguay round, agriculture was exempted from trade liberalisation in all multilateral trade agreements. The Uruguay round reformed and simplified the political economy of agricultural trade without really liberalising agricultural trade. If trade is indeed opened up in the coming decade, this will cause major shifts in production and trade. Regions with a comparative advantage in agriculture and food (i.e. the Americas, Australia, New Zealand) are likely to benefit at the cost of the other regions (Western Europe, Japan, China, India). Figure 3 shows the effects of worldwide reductions in agricultural and food tariffs and producer subsidies on the farm and food trade balance.

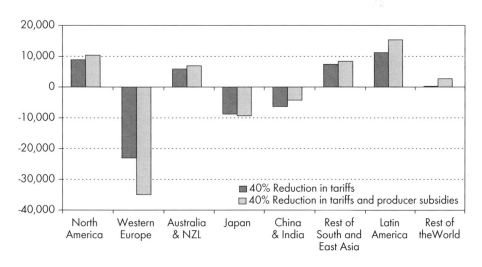

*Figure 3. Impact of trade liberalisation scenarios in agriculture and food (Mln. USD) (Hertel et al., 2004).*

## Foreign direct investment

Contemporary international processes involve more than trade. Since at least the 1990s, growth in foreign direct investment (FDI) has outpaced growth in international trade (see Table 2). Many OECD countries sell more products through foreign affiliates than through exports (Blonigen, 2005; OECD, 2006).

FDI is becoming more important, and since we do not know that much about it, further study is warranted. It may be used as a substitute for trade, or it may be complementary to trade. Economic theory does not provide a clear explanation of the exact nature of the relationship between FDI and trade. One thing we know for sure is that FDI influences trade. In this respect, one *Many OECD countries* can make a distinction between horizontal FDI and *sell more products* vertical FDI (Blonigen, 2005). The former is used as *through foreign affiliates* a mechanism to sell in different geographical markets *than through exports* in order, for example, to circumvent trade barriers or transport costs. In this case, FDI replaces exports (see Figure 4A). Firms may also use one host country as a production platform to serve a group of countries, for instance the European Union. In this case, FDI reduces the exports of the home country to the benefit of host country B (Figure 4B). Vertical FDI is used to transfer part of the production process to a cheaper location, in

Table 2. Worldwide growth in food and beverages: 1990-2004 (UNCTAD, WTO and EU).

| Economic activity | Annual growth | |
| --- | --- | --- |
| | Developed countries | Developing countries |
| Production | 3.5% | n.a. |
| International trade | 5.2% | 5.4% |
| FDI | 9.8% | 10.8% |

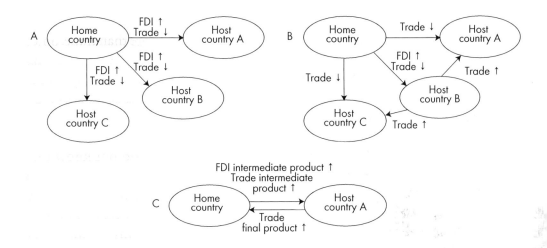

*Figure 4. A: Horizontal FDI replaces trade; B: Platform FDI replaces and shifts trade patterns; C: Vertical FDI creates trade patterns.*

which case, FDI may lead to trade in intermediate products (see Figure 4C). The home country invests in host country A and exports to and imports from that country. Of course, in reality, more complex FDI and trade patterns are observed.

The empirical literature has not yet established what the dominant types of FDI are, let alone how FDI influences trade. It is suggested that there is more evidence for horizontal FDI and the platform hypothesis than for vertical FDI (Blonigen, 2005). This may well be because most FDI occurs between developed countries with comparable cost structures. In the future, when more FDI flows to developing countries, vertical FDI may become more important. Because we do not as yet know much about FDI – or about any other internationalisation strategy apart from trade – future research will no doubt try to find out why certain types of FDI occur, how FDI influences trade, and how it benefits both home and host countries.

## The open world market and a few of its consequences

For the food supply chain in OECD countries, the opening up of markets provides opportunities as well as challenges. Competition on price and product R&D will become more intense. As a result, profits will fall and both food companies and markets will restructure. Falling profit rates promote industry concentration and the return of multinationals to their core activities. John Sutton (1991; 2003) argues that economic integration intensifies price competition. Because profit margins fall as a result, firms need higher volumes to cover fixed expenses such as set-up costs and advertising and R&D outlays. Moreover, advertising and R&D outlays may very well go up, because firms tend to spend more on advertising and product R&D in larger markets. The multinationals surviving these competition processes will become bigger in fewer markets.

Increasing price competition will put further pressure on food supply chains to bring down costs. Costs will be reduced by promoting production on demand thereby reducing lead times and inventories throughout the supply chain. Costs will also be reduced by reallocating inventories during the production and distribution process. Food shipments will change ownership and destination during their journey. These processes will be made possible by the introduction of such new information technologies as mobile logistics, RFID, telematics and wireless broadband, by supply chain coordination (Electronic Data Interchange) and by the introduction of new storage techniques. The latter will enable the shipment of fresh produce from all over the world. At the same time, production technologies will become more modular. This will enable food companies to slice up the supply chain by eliminating or outsourcing supply chain activities and supply chain links. In an international context, the slicing up of activities has consequences for vertical FDI (see above and the chapter by Arjen van Witteloostuijn in this volume).

*Increasing price competition will put further pressure on food supply chains to bring down costs*

The opening up of world markets provides both a challenge and an opportunity for SMEs, especially because production technologies are becoming modular. On the one hand, global competition becomes so pervasive that SMEs – even in the most remote rural areas – face competition from both large corporations and SMEs from all around the world. On the other hand, because the production technologies of the future are modular and flexible rather than large scale and vertically integrated, SMEs have the opportunity to pick up a part of a worldwide supply chain and develop a comparative advantage in that part.

The opening up of markets also provides ample opportunities for Western food companies. First, the demand for food increases in the developing world. Second, Western multinationals have a first mover advantage relative to their competitors in developing countries. Western multinationals own brands with established reputations. Third, Western food companies have access to cutting-edge technologies including research facilities. Western multinationals may be in a good position to profit from demand growth in developing countries. However, this does not imply that employees in Western countries benefit as well. Take Unilever. Worldwide employment at Unilever fell from 306,000 employees to 189,000 (-38%) from 1996 till 2006. The sharpest reduction has occurred in Europe (-53%).

## Social responsibility

The fourth and final development discussed in this chapter has social responsibility at its core. Social responsibility is one of the main new arguments influencing contemporary food choice. There is a small but growing group of consumers who base their buying habits on, for example, ethical values regarding the environment, animal welfare and the working conditions of farmers and employees in developing countries. Responsible consumer behaviour has extended the realm of responsible citizenship to a new activity: food choice and consumption. Consequently, both consumers and food retailers are showing interest in the production and distribution process. This explains, for instance, the proliferation of labels and certifications indicating whether food is healthy, environmentally friendly, GMO-free or fair trade. The impact of responsible consumerism on food production and distribution goes beyond the small number of consumers who buy on ethical grounds, because the general concern in society with respect to ethical issues is much broader. Indeed, issues such as health (obesity), animal welfare and environmental care remain public issues as well. It will be a major challenge to match public and private responsibilities.

*It is far from clear whether trade liberalisation has a beneficial or a detrimental net effect on the environment*

Within the context of international economic relations, ethical issues are also put on the agenda. This holds, for instance, for competition, the environment, animal welfare, labour conditions, technical standards, investments and intellectual property rights. Some of these issues (i.e. environment, technical standards, intellectual property rights) are already on the WTO agenda, and some of them are not (competition, investment). In all these issues, the relationship between developed and developing countries plays a key role. These issues influence developing countries' opportunities of market access and income distribution between developed and developing countries.

At this moment, within the WTO, the relationship between trade and the environment is one of the issues being addressed. This provides the opportunity to discuss such matters as why there has been until now so little regulation of international trade with respect to environmental issues (apart from threatened species and biodiversity), or the fact that we have little systematic knowledge about the relationship between agricultural trade and the environment in either developed or developing countries. It is far from clear whether trade liberalisation has a beneficial or a detrimental net effect on the environment. Moreover, even if the relationship between trade and the environment is negative on net, it is questionable whether international trade negotiations are the most appropriate place to discuss environmental issues. After all, trade measures would, at most, be second-best solutions.

Within the WTO framework, countries are allowed to specify sanitary and phytosanitary measures (SPS Agreement) to protect persons, flora, fauna, the environment and consumers. Although countries are encouraged to base their SPS measures on international standards, they may apply higher standards. There is a debate about whether SPS measures constitute a trade barrier for developing countries. Gretchen Stanton (2004) argues that the SPS Agreement has increased the transparency and predictability of SPS measures. Moreover, the Agreement reduces the scope for trade protection, because the importer – rather than the exporter – has to justify the sanitary and phytosanitary effects of additional measures before the WTO. Both developed and developing countries benefit from this achievement. However, Spencer Henson *et al.* (2004) argue that developing countries lack the public infrastructure that is required to participate in the SPS Agreement. If that is true, case law will be dominated by developed countries.

## Social concerns, private standards and prices

As will be discussed in more detail in the chapter by Barbara Fliess, it can be stated that because consumers and NGOs forward their social concerns, food companies take on their responsibilities and develop CSR policies. Food retailers take the lead in introducing social responsibility in the food supply chain. Apart from addressing the responsibilities they have with respect to their own operations, food retailers also pass on social concerns to their suppliers. Suppliers are carefully selected in order to guarantee a minimum level of social responsibility. For this reason, food retailers develop private standards with respect to food safety and social and environmental production conditions. Private standards typically exceed public standards and thus develop into the more relevant standard (Fulponi, 2007). However, Pepijn van der Port argues further on in this book that private standards heavily depend on a body of public standards. Private standards address social concerns, but may do so at a price. Private standards may inhibit smallholder access from developing countries to high-volume, high-value added food supply chains in developed countries. Private standards require investments in capital, technology, management and a public infrastructure to accommodate these investments. So far, there is little and mixed evidence that private standards impede smallholder access (Swinnen, 2007). In order to meet the demand for ethical production and consumption, food retailers also broaden the product assortment with responsible products such as organics or fair trade products.

The sustainability issue not only affects the food supply chain through the development of ever more stringent private standards, but also through scarcity and the price mechanism. This holds notably for natural resources and the environment (for an assessment of the major sustainability in livestock production, see the chapter by Henning Steinfeld in this volume). The price of agricultural commodities and energy may be expected to go up, because natural resources (oil and gas) are depleted and the environment (land) degrades. The price of agricultural commodities and energy may also go up due to further public regulation. As a result of both developments, supplies may become more expensive in the decades to come, at least more expensive than they otherwise would have been.

# The biofuels boom: implications for world food markets

*Dileep K. Birur, Thomas W. Hertel and Wallace E. Tyner*

This chapter evaluates the impact of the recent biofuels boom on world food markets. We begin with an analysis of the origins of the bio-fuel boom – from a US perspective. We conclude by predicting a slowing of the ethanol boom in the US, as production satiates the high-value demand for ethanol as an additive so that future growth hinges of its ability to substitute for petroleum products on an energy equivalent basis. This transition is reflected in the elimination of the price premium for ethanol, the price of which has dropped sharply recently. This, combined with higher corn prices, has served to curtail most plans for new ethanol capacity – at least for the present.

Our prospective analysis of the impacts of the biofuels boom on food markets focuses on the 2006-2010 time period, during which existing investments in the US, and new mandates in the EU are expected to substantially increase the share of agricultural products (e.g. corn in the US, oilseeds in the EU and sugar in Brazil) utilised by the biofuels sector. In the US, this share could double from 2006 levels, while the share of oilseeds going to biodiesel in the EU could triple. We expect such expansion to lead to a doubling of US corn and EU oilseed prices, from 2006 levels, thereby sharply reducing exports, while boosting imports. In the EU, the majority of the new demand for oilseeds due to biodiesel expansion is met by imports, with EU oilseed import volume rising by more than $4 billion.

These increases in biofuels demand in the US and EU have a profound impact on the pattern of global agricultural production and land use. Wheat and soybean acreage and production falls in the US, along with other crops, livestock and forestry land use. In the EU, acreage devoted to oilseeds rises by 21 precent. This reallocation of land use is rather similar in Canada and Brazil, where oilseeds production also responds strongly to higher world prices, as does coarse grains production in Canada, and sugarcane production in Brazil. This puts considerable pressure on agriculture and forest lands throughout the world. In Brazil, agriculture is expected to expand into forest lands – particularly in the most productive agro-ecological zones (AEZ).

In addition to altering the global agricultural landscape, these developments in US and EU biofuels use have a significant impact on energy markets. Solely as a result of these 'mandates', the US trade balance for petroleum products improves by about $6 billion. This is largely offset by deterioration in the US agricultural trade balance. In the EU, the deterioration in the agricultural trade balance is much larger, but this is compensated for by a strong increase in the net exports of manufactures and services. Overall, current developments in the US and EU biofuels markets, including the European Commission's 5.75% biofuel mandate, are likely to have significant, and lasting impacts on the global pattern of agricultural production and trade.

## Booming biofuels

Interest in biofuels initially came about in the late 1970s as OPEC reduced crude oil supply on the world market and fuel prices increased substantially. Both the US and Brazil launched ethanol programmes during this period. The US, EU, and Brazil all have subsidies or regulations promoting biofuels. In Brazil and the US, ethanol is the predominant fuel, and in the EU, it is biodiesel. Until 2006, Brazil was the global leader in ethanol production, but with the developments in world oil markets plus US domestic policy described below, the US overtook Brazil in 2006. However, it is cheaper to produce ethanol from sugarcane, the resource used in Brazil, than to produce it from corn, the raw material currently used in the US. The energy balance also is much more positive for sugarcane based ethanol than for ethanol from corn. Therefore, in the absence of government intervention, we would expect Brazilian ethanol to be dominant.

The European Union Biofuels Directive requires that member states should realise 5.75% share of biofuels on the liquid fuels market by 2010 (Commission of the European Communities, 2003). Biodiesel production has been a more recent addition to the global biofuels scene, as shown in Figure 1 (note the difference in scales for the two types of biofuels). Germany is the largest producer (798 million gallons[1] constituting about 54% of EU-27's total biodiesel production in 2006) followed by France (15%), Italy (9%), United Kingdom (4%), Austria (2.5%), Poland (2.4%), Czech Republic (2.2%), Spain (2%), and others (9%) (European Biodiesel Board). The spectacular growth in the German market was the result of a very favourable legislation granting a total tax exemption for biofuels, which has recently been rescinded.

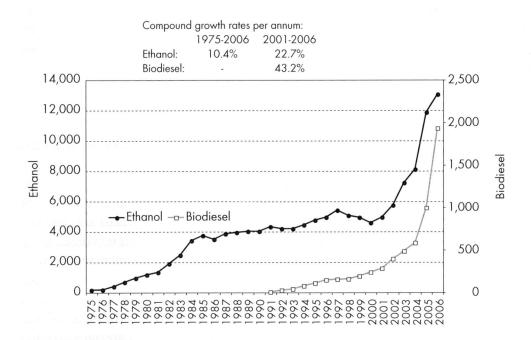

Figure 1. World Production of Ethanol and Biodiesel (million gallons) (Earth Policy Institute, 2006; FAPRI, 2007; EBB, 2007).

---

[1] One US gallon is 3.785 litres.

Dileep K. Birur, Thomas W. Hertel and Wallace E. Tyner

## Growth in ethanol production

In the US, subsidisation of ethanol began with the Energy Policy Act of 1978. At the time, the main arguments that were used to justify the subsidy were enhanced farm income and, to a lesser extent, energy security. In 1990, the Clean Air Act was passed, which required vendors of gasoline to have a minimum oxygen percentage in their product. Adding oxygen enables the fuel to burn cleaner, so a cleaner environment became an important justification for ethanol subsidies. Since ethanol has a larger percentage of oxygen than standard gasoline, or methyl tertiary butyl ether (MTBE), its main competitor in the additive market, the demand for ethanol as an additive offered good prospects. However, MTBE is produced from petroleum products by oil companies and was generally cheaper than ethanol, so it continued to be the favored way of meeting the oxygen requirements throughout the 1990s.

This growth in MTBE use was, however, short-lived, as it began to crop up in water supplies in several regions in the country. Since MTBE is highly toxic, it was subsequently banned by about 20 states. That left ethanol as the major source of added oxygen in those states by the early 2000s. Two years ago, Congress debated and ultimately passed the Energy Policy Act of 2005. During the debate, oil companies lobbied to be given exemption from legal liability from MTBE issues. Congress did not grant the legal liability exemption but did agree to remove the oxygen requirements leaving oil companies free to meet the clean air rules in any way they saw fit (ethanol, reformulated gasoline, etc.). The US Environmental Protection Agency issued rules eliminating the oxygen requirement as of May 2006. Oil companies generally believed they had legal cover for MTBE so long as the government was requiring them to meet a minimum oxygen requirement. But with the removal of the oxygen requirement, companies no longer had that legal cover and made a big push to use ethanol in its place. This resulted in a sharp price spike in the ethanol market in summer 2006. Since that time, the price of ethanol has been falling, as the demand for ethanol as an additive has become satiated, and ethanol is increasingly priced for its energy content.

During the 20 years between 1983 and 2003 the US ethanol subsidy varied between 50 and 60 cents per gallon. Over that time period, crude oil ranged between $10 and $30 per barrel with a couple of short exceptions. Figure 2 shows the growth of US ethanol production and coincident decline in MTBE production during the 1992-2006 period. The subsidy was sufficient to ensure a profit except for a few months in 1996 when corn prices reached record high levels. However, the subsidy was not enough to create rapid growth in the industry. That subsidy, together with oil in the $10 to $30 range was sufficient to permit steady growth in ethanol production from about 430 million gallons in 1984 to about 3.4 billion gallons in 2004. In other words, production grew by about 149 million gallons per year over this period. In 2004, the crude oil price began its steep climb to around $70/bbl, and it has been hovering between

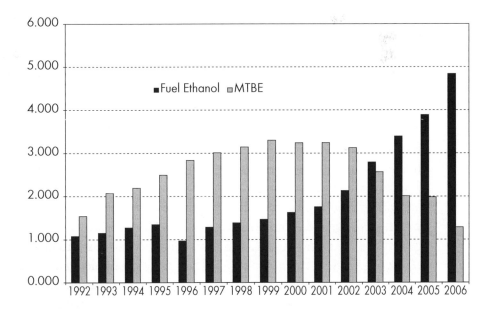

*Figure 2. Production of Fuel Ethanol and MTBE in the US (billion gallons) (Energy Information Administration, US Department of Energy).*

Dileep K. Birur, Thomas W. Hertel and Wallace E. Tyner

$60 and $80/bbl in recent months. This rapid increase in the crude price, together with an exogenously fixed ethanol subsidy, led to a tremendous boom in the construction of ethanol plants. Ethanol production in 2005 was about 4 billion gallons, and it will likely surpass 11 billion gallons in 2008. At this point, we expect it to make use of over 30% of the US corn crop. Production will have grown by about 1.9 billion gallons per year over that four year period compared with 149 million gallons in the preceding years. It has been, then, the combination of high oil prices, a shift in the demand for ethanol as a fuel additive, and a subsidy that was keyed to $20 oil that has led to this boom in US ethanol production.

## Will the US boom last?

We can illustrate these three key drivers of recent growth in the ethanol market with the break-even graphs shown in Figure 3. The graphs illustrate at what combinations of crude oil and corn prices revenues equal costs under three different assumptions. (1) The top line in the graph assumes there is no ethanol subsidy and that ethanol is priced on an energy equivalent basis with gasoline. (2) The second line assumes no subsidy again but that there is a 35 cent per gallon additive value for ethanol. (3) And the third line adds the 51 cent per gallon federal ethanol subsidy (the assumptions and econometric estimations used in producing this graph are contained in Tyner and Taheripour, 2007).

For $60/bbl oil, the energy, additive, and additive plus subsidy breakeven corn prices are $2.01, $3.12, and $4.72 per bushel (bu.) respectively. If there is no additive value, the energy plus subsidy breakeven is $3.62/bu. at $60/bbl oil. Clearly, so long as ethanol has a considerable additive value, ethanol production will continue to grow until corn reaches about $5/bu. But if ethanol is priced on an energy equivalent basis (as it would be for E-85 blends for example) and the current policy regime remains in place, then investment would cease at corn prices not much higher than they are today. We expect that the additive market will be saturated in the near future, so energy equivalent pricing is much more likely for the future. This

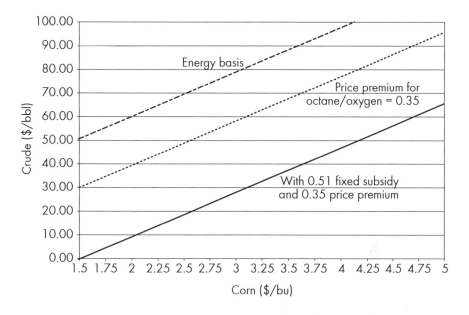

Figure 3. Breakeven corn and crude prices with ethanol on energy and premium bases plus ethanol subsidy (Tyner and Taheripour, 2007).

suggests that the biofuel boom in the US may soon be coming to an end.

## Consequences for corn

The ethanol boom has, in turn, led to a rapid run-up in corn and other commodity prices in 2006-2007, as land has been diverted from these crops to corn – soybeans, in particular. The run-up in commodity prices has fueled debate over the food-fuel issue and raised questions on the extent to which renewable fuels can be supplied from corn alone. In a year's time the price of corn went from $2.20/bu. to $3.50/bu. or higher – an increase of 60%. Soybean prices went up even more as there were massive shifts in soybean acreage to corn. This is not to say, however, that food prices will increase in like proportion. Corn is used primarily as an animal feed, with the proportion varying by animal species. Poultry meat and eggs are facing the largest shock as corn constitutes about two-thirds of the poultry ration. As a consequence, the total cost of producing poultry meat and eggs has increased by about 15% over this period. It is unlikely, however, that all this cost increase can be passed on to consumers. For other commodities, the cost increase is smaller, and it is substantially smaller for the total consumer food bill. Recent estimates put the consumer food bill increase to date, due to corn ethanol, between 1.1 and 1.8% (Tokgoz *et al.*, 2007). But in terms of the annual food bill, it is estimated that US consumers will pay $22 billion more for food due to biofuels (Alexander and Hurt, 2007).

As indicated above, corn ethanol production is likely to reach 11-12 billion gallons in 2008. In a remarkable response to this increased demand and favourable prices, US corn acreage went from 78 million in 2006 to 92 million acres in 2007. Most of that acreage increase came at the expense of soybeans, thereby driving soybean prices substantially higher. How much higher will ethanol production go and what will be the determining factors? Most industry and agriculture experts (Tokgoz *et al.*, 2007) figure corn ethanol production will top out around 15 billion gallons by 2012. This would constitute 10% of projected US gasoline consumption (US Energy Information Administration) by volume and about 7% on an energy equivalent basis. The volumetric and energy equivalent shares are different because ethanol contains about 68% of the energy of gasoline per unit volume. Miles per gallon, at least in the short run, will be determined by energy content, so consumers are unlikely to be willing to pay more for ethanol than its energy equivalence to gasoline once it is widely known that ethanol blends yield lower fuel economy than gasoline alone. This suggests that there is limited scope for increasing the price of ethanol unless petroleum prices rise substantially.

Unless current high oil prices are sustained, the US biofuel boom based on corn will gradually come to a halt, with total capacity settling in at about 15 billion gallons – nearly double current levels – and conveniently at the level dictated for 2015 by the 2007 US Energy Policy and Security Act. Although factoring in the capacity already nearing completion, ethanol demand in the US represents a very substantial claim on corn production. When coupled with mandates in the EU, and potential subsidies for biofuels elsewhere around the world, this could have a very substantial impact on the long run patterns of global food and agricultural production and trade. The remainder of this chapter seeks to investigate this link between increased biofuel production and food trade.

## Mandates in the EU and US

As noted earlier, both the EU and the US have announced biofuel targets. As seen from Table 1, the share of biofuels in liquids for transport on energy basis constituted only 1.91% and 1.53%, respectively for the US and EU during 2006. In the EU, the goal is to reach 5.75% of energy used in transportation by 2010. Compared to reported biofuel use in 2006, this entails a 281% increase in biofuels' share of liquid fuel consumption. In the US, the Energy Policy and Security Act of 2007 targets 15 billion gallons of ethanol by 2015. However, capacity is already in place or under construction to nearly reach this target. Indeed, we estimate that ethanol capacity will reach 13.4 billion gallons by 2010 which constitutes 4.62% of liquid fuels for transportation on energy basis. This amounts to a 176% boost in ethanol production for 2010 (see Table 1). We adopt this as our

*In the EU, the goal is to reach 5.75% of energy used in transportation by 2010; compared to reported biofuel use in 2006, this entails a 281% increase in biofuels' share of liquid fuel consumption*

*Table 1. Biofuels mandates in the EU and US.*

|  |  | US | EU27 |
|---|---|---|---|
| 2006 | Current production (million gallons) | 5,240 | 1,888 |
|  | Share of biofuels in liquids for transport | 1.91% | 1.53% |
| 2010 | Bio-fuels mandate for 2010 (million gallons) | 13,429 | 7,200 |
|  | Share of biofuels in liquids for transport | 4.62% | 5.75% |
| % Change from 2006 to 2010 |  | 176 | 281 |

target in this 'mandates' simulation[2]. Importantly, we *do not* include bio-diesel in this US mandate as it is produced from soybeans in the US, which is regarded as an expensive source of feedstock for biodiesel. Due to its non-viability, biodiesel production is not likely to grow much and hence we assume no contribution from biodiesel to meet the mandate.

## Biofuel growth and US food market: a 2010 scenario

The strong expansion in ethanol production envisioned under our 2010 scenario more than doubles the share of US corn going to ethanol production – from 16% of total sales in our 2006 data base, to 38% of total sales in the projected 2010 data base. This increased share comes primarily at the expense of corn going to feed use and exports, which decline by 6% and 48%, respectively. The share of US coarse grains production exported falls from 23% in our 2006 baseline to 10% under the mandates scenario, as the price of US corn nearly doubles under this scenario. The change in output following the implementation of the mandate, is given in terms of domestic and exports components (Table 2). In US, only

---

[2] By way of background information, a few words about the methodology that underpins our analysis are illustrative. In order to draw the link between developments in US biofuels and food trade, we need a formal modelling framework. And we aim to simultaneously include the EU biofuel mandates in this analysis. To do so, we require a global model that links energy markets with biofuels, biofuels with agricultural markets, and agricultural markets with land use and international trade (a detailed description of the GTAP-BIO model used in this analysis is offered in Birur *et al.*, 2007). Key features include: (1) the incorporation of biofuels into the GTAP-E global energy data base and model; (2) extension of the latter to a broader set of regions and agricultural commodities, and (3) the addition of Agro-ecological Zones (AEZs) for each of the land using sectors, following the methodology outlined in Tom Hertel *et al.* (2008). In the US, we distinguish between the demand for ethanol as an additive, and the demand for ethanol as an energy substitute. Extension of the energy model to encompass agricultural products to highlight key agricultural exporters is critical for understanding the food market impacts of the biofuels boom. And finally, the more refined treatment of the global land data base is essential since corn, for example, competes with different crops in different parts of the US. As noted above, the expansion of corn for use in ethanol has had a much larger impact on soybeans than on other crops. By disaggregating the global land endowments by AEZ, we are able to take account of this dimension of land competition. We validate the model by simulating it over the historical period: 2001-2006. And our analysis of biofuel mandates takes 2006 as its starting point.

Table 2. Impact of biofuels mandates implementation on agricultural markets in the US, EU, and Brazil.

| | US | | | EU | | | Brazil | | |
| | Change in Output (%) | | | Change in Output (%) | | | Change in Output (%) | | |
| | Total = | Domestic | +Exports | Total = | Domestic | +Exports | Total = | Domestic | +Exports |
|---|---|---|---|---|---|---|---|---|---|
| Coarse grains | 13.8 | 24.6 | -10.7 | 3.6 | 4.8 | -1.2 | 6.5 | -1.3 | 7.7 |
| Other grains | -12.5 | -1.8 | -10.7 | -10.8 | -4.7 | -6.0 | -6.2 | -6.2 | 0.0 |
| Oilseeds | -4.5 | -1.7 | -2.8 | 26.4 | 38.4 | -12.0 | 16.1 | -0.7 | 16.8 |
| Sugarcane | -4.2 | -4.2 | 0.0 | -3.3 | -3.3 | 0.0 | 3.7 | 3.7 | 0.0 |
| Livestock | -5.1 | -4.2 | -0.8 | -3.2 | -2.7 | -0.5 | -2.9 | -2.9 | 0.0 |
| Forestry | -1.5 | -0.9 | -0.6 | -2.5 | -1.6 | -0.9 | -1.3 | -1.2 | -0.1 |
| Other food products | -1.3 | -1.4 | 0.1 | -1.6 | -1.3 | -0.3 | -2.5 | -1.2 | -1.3 |
| Processed livestock | -3.3 | -2.7 | -0.5 | -2.2 | -1.6 | -0.5 | -3.8 | -1.3 | -2.5 |
| Other agriculture | -4.1 | -3.6 | -0.5 | -3.9 | -2.6 | -1.4 | -3.8 | -1.6 | -2.2 |

production of coarse grains goes up by 14% which mainly comes from 25% increase in demand for domestic use, coupled with decline in exports by 11% (first row of Table 2). The production of all other agricultural commodities goes down substantially. Meanwhile, the share of production going to feedstuffs falls from 43% to 37%. This contraction of other uses, coupled with a 14% increase in corn output, permits ethanol production to rise by 174%, as mandated in our 2006-2010 simulation scenario.

Next to a modest increase in yields as a result of more intensive cultivation practices, the increase in corn output is met largely by increases in land used for coarse grains. Figure 4 shows a map of the world, with the percentage change in coarse grains acreage, by agro-ecological zone (AEZ) and region. The percentage increase in acreage varies by AEZ, with the rise in the US Corn Belt being about 10%. The largest percentage changes in corn acreage (up to 25%) are in the less-productive AEZs which contribute little to national coarse grains output. Thus the productivity-weighted rise in coarse grains acreage is close to the Corn Belt figure and is just 11%. Meanwhile, oilseeds acreage in the US falls, as land is shifted from soybeans to corn.

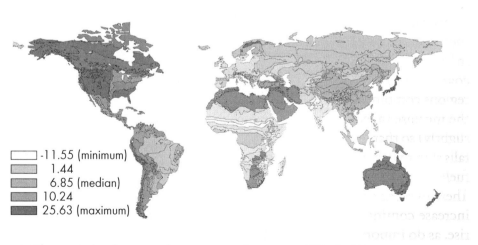

-11.55 (minimum)
1.44
6.85 (median)
10.24
25.63 (maximum)

Figure 4. Change in land area under coarse grains across AEZs (in %).

## Impacts of biofuel growth: EU and international trade

Next we turn to the projected impacts in the EU. Here, the mandate represents a much larger change in percentage terms. The 281% increase in biofuel production is largely biodiesel, and this generates a strong demand for oilseeds, the production of which rises by 26% in response to a doubling of oilseed prices in the EU. This increase in production is far less than the required rise in use by the biodiesel sector, which is about triple this amount (nearly 80% of current production), and the difference is made up by increased imports of oilseeds as well as the virtual elimination of exports by the EU oilseeds sector. Thus the EU biofuel mandate has a very strong impact on international agricultural trade.

The anticipated impacts on land use and outputs in the oilseeds sector is shown in Table 2. In order to meet the increased domestic production of oilseeds, oilseeds acreage rises across the board, with the increases ranging from 7% to more than 30%, depending on the AEZ, with the overall productivity-weighted average for land used in oilseeds rising by 12%. This land comes out of other grains, livestock and forestry, as the coarse grains and sugar acreage expands slightly, the price rises following the ethanol boom.

Apart from the domestic impacts in the US and EU, it is clear that these effects will be felt around the world. The individual columns in Table 3 report the changes in import volumes ($US million) for coarse grains and oilseeds by the EU and US, as well as all other regions combined. The decline in US coarse grains exports exceeds the increase in exports from all other regions (EU exports decline slightly) so that the total volume of trade for this group of products falls slightly. On the other hand, global trade in oilseeds rises sharply, fueled by the EU oilseeds imports increase of more than $4 billion. These oilseeds are sourced from around the world, with the largest increase coming from Brazil. Imports of ethanol from Brazil also rise, as do imports of grains and livestock products.

Table 3. Bilateral Trade Impacts due to US-EU biofuel expansion: 2006-2010 ($ millions, change in volume evaluated at initial market prices).

| Exporters: | Coarse Grains | | | | Oilseeds | | | |
|---|---|---|---|---|---|---|---|---|
| | Importers | | | Total exports | Importers | | | Total exports |
| | USA | EU | Rest of the world | | USA | EU | Rest of the world | |
| US | - | -53 | -2,658 | -2,711 | - | 625 | -981 | -356 |
| Canada | 169 | 3 | 36 | 208 | 10 | 176 | 129 | 315 |
| EU | 41 | - | -125 | -84 | -2 | - | -187 | -189 |
| Brazil | 0 | 48 | 141 | 189 | 0 | 1,210 | -146 | 1,064 |
| China-Hong Kong | 1 | 7 | 372 | 380 | 2 | 326 | 128 | 456 |
| Rest of the Americas | 93 | 48 | 269 | 410 | 4 | 476 | 164 | 644 |
| FSU[1] and Rest of Europe | 9 | 123 | 289 | 421 | 4 | 641 | 40 | 685 |
| Middle East and North Africa | 26 | 31 | 266 | 323 | 8 | 294 | 70 | 372 |
| Rest of Asia | 6 | 6 | 42 | 54 | 38 | 284 | 255 | 577 |
| Oceania | 0 | 1 | 140 | 141 | 0 | 72 | -7 | 65 |
| Total imports | 345 | 214 | -1,228 | -669 | 64 | 4,104 | -535 | 3,633 |

[1] Former Soviet Union.

Of course in the aggregate, global trade must balance, and each region's current account must be equated to its capital account. Since the latter changes little as a result of the biofuel mandates, any increase in regional import values must be largely offset by an increase in export values. Table 4 reports the changes in trade balance (2006-2010) for US, EU and the rest of the world as a consequence of the biofuel mandates in the US and EU. Thus the US farm and food sector shows a negative change in trade balance ($3.6 billion). This is offset by a positive change in the trade balance for oil and oil products ($6.3 billion), as biofuels substitute for petroleum products. In addition, there is an increase in biofuel imports and a (net) positive change in the trade balance for other manufactures and services. In the aggregate, the US trade balance improves slightly as a result of these mandates, and the terms of trade improve, as the price of oil imports falls and the prices of agricultural exports rise. The story in the EU is quite similar to the US in sign, but the magnitude of the agri-food trade balance deterioration is much larger in the EU (-$15.3 billion). The improvement in oil products trade balance is half that in the US (+$3.0 billion). The difference is made up by a much stronger improvement in the trade balance of other sectors such as manufactures and services ($12.1 billion). Here, the terms of trade deteriorate slightly.

*Table 4. Change in Trade Balance due to biofuels mandates: 2006-2010 ($ billions).*

|  | US | EU | Rest of the World | Total |
|---|---|---|---|---|
| Agri and Food | -3.634 | -15.341 | 19.35 | 0.375 |
| Biofuels | -1.154 | -0.298 | 1.448 | -0.004 |
| Oil Products | 6.326 | 3.003 | -9.107 | 0.222 |
| Other | 0.684 | 12.155 | -13.43 | -0.591 |
| Total change in trade balance | 2.22 | -0.48 | -1.74 | 0 |

# Part 3

## 'Software'
## becoming 'hardware'

# Informing consumers about social and environmental conditions of globalised production[3]

*Barbara Fliess*

While price, safety and product quality remain leading criteria motivating purchasing decisions in OECD markets for food and manufactured goods, consumers increasingly attach importance to how companies from which they buy conduct their business. Developments also show that the voluntary adoption of socially responsible practices is spreading in the private sector in response to demand from consumers and other stakeholders.

At the interface of these two trends lies the question explored in this chapter: how do consumers obtain information enabling them to choose products made under acceptable social and environmental conditions surrounding their production? The chapter describes tools that are available and are used for informing consumer choice and takes two products – fish and cut flowers – as case studies documenting their use. In the specific agro-food markets of fisheries and cut flowers processors and retailers have found themselves under growing pressure from consumers and other stakeholders to conduct their business and manage transnational supply chains in ways that respect the environment and provide acceptable working conditions.

Faced with markets that are supplied by increasingly globally organised commodity and production networks involving countries at different stages of development, better off consumers in the developed world not only demand that products are safe but also pay increasing attention to how a company and its international subcontractors treat employees and impacts on the environment. Although corporate

---

[3] This chapter draws on a 2006 study carried out by OECD, which Hyung-Jong Lee, Olivia L. Dubreuil and Osvaldo Agatiello co-authored.

social responsibility (CSR) refers to voluntary business activities responding to a range of societal concerns (workplace, social, anti-corruption, technology-related and environmental issues), the focus here is consumer concerns about environmental and social conditions of production and tools for informing consumer choice. This chapter does not address the broader political dimension of CSR or the actual impact of CSR activities or reflect the debate in a comprehensive manner that includes all stakeholders, in developed and developing countries.

## Consumer interest in CSR and purchasing behaviour

There is ample evidence that consumers of the developed world have become more aware in recent years of the way companies conduct their business, both at home and abroad, and interested in CSR, including the issue of socially responsible production. A consistent finding of polls taken in the last decade in developed country markets is that a large number of consumers affirm that whether or not companies are committed to social responsibility is important to them. The proportion of the British public saying that CSR is very important in their purchasing decisions doubled from 1997 to 2001, to 46% (Dawkins and Lewis, 2003), and across 12 European countries 70% of the public deemed a company's commitments to CSR an important consideration in their product choice (MORI, 2000). Likewise, 92% of Canadians report that the more socially and environmentally responsible a company is, the more likely they are to buy from it (Ipsos Reid, 2003). According to GlobeScan's *CSR Monitor* survey in 2002 of consumers in 20 countries, 42% of respondents in North America and 25% in Europe reported not buying the products of companies whose social and environmental performance is perceived to be poor. Although dependent on individuals' level of income and other factors, a substantial number of consumers seem willing to pay a premium for products derived from production matching their environmental or social values.

*Consumers of the developed world have become more aware in recent years of the way companies conduct their business*

Looking at actual consumption, in most OECD countries products originating from socially responsible production enjoy still relatively modest but usually growing market shares. This is illustrated by the rapid growth in recent years of Fair Trade coffee, bananas and other products, of free-range eggs, and the even more impressive transition of organic foods from small- to industrial-scale production and supermarket retailing in a matter of ten years. At the same time, market research reveals a gap between what consumers say and do: many say that they care but for various reasons do not purchase based on their stated preferences.

For example, market research finds that for most consumers price and product quality are the most important purchasing criteria, and that only a minority of consumers place CSR anywhere near the top on their list of decision-making criteria for shopping (Cowe and Williams, 2000; Doane, 2005; Imug, 2003). While there are other reasons for the discrepancy – for example, some consumers do not act on their stated preferences because they think that their individual purchase decisions will not influence corporate product policies and business practices – one important factor enabling consumers to distinguish among products or brands based on CSR criteria is knowledge. Opinion polls show that a large number of consumers do not feel well informed about CSR, including companies' production practices (MORI, 2003; Alter Eco, 2005). This suggests that more information and effective communication can engage more consumers who state that they care about CSR, to purchase accordingly, and more generally improve buyer awareness of what companies are actually doing in this area. For companies that adopt CSR programmes in response to a changing landscape of consumer expectations or other reasons (e.g. managing risk and building a positive reputation, protecting human capital assets, or avoiding regulation), the low level of the public's knowledge of corporate CSR practices documented by opinion polls suggest that their CSR programmes and accomplishments are simply not being registered by consumers.

Closely linked to consumers' need for information in order to act on their stated preferences is the issue of product availability and easy access. There may not be enough visible criteria available for consumers to actually distinguish between more or less socially responsible products (AGENDA, 2004). Also, consumers have buying habits and are less inclined to purchase CSR or any other preferred products if these products are not conveniently available but require special efforts, for instance visiting a specialised store. When a store promotes CSR products by putting them in highly visible spots, it can clearly reveal CSR to consumers.

*When a store promotes CSR products by putting them in highly visible spots, it can clearly reveal CSR to consumers*

Conversely, activities such as quality agreements with other companies in the supply chain that include CSR principles and commitments are not directly visible to consumers. This difference in visibility can affect CSR perceptions (Van Herpen *et al.*, 2003). In Europe, an important recent development boosting sales of Fair Trade Certified products has been their move into the mainstream marketing channels of the large retail chains. The arrival of Fair Trade brands such as Max Havelaar on the shelves of French supermarkets and hypermarkets has coincided with a notable increase in Fair Trade food sales.

## Informing consumers: certification and labelling schemes

Perhaps most visible among the tools for reaching consumers and communicating about CSR practices are voluntary certification and labelling schemes. Certification by private parties has proliferated in recent years especially in the field of food safety and quality but is undertaken also to increase consumers' awareness of social and environmental issues. Certification systems can vary in design and operation, but generally contain certain key elements: firstly, certifying the firm when its performance meets a set standard, and, secondly, certifying the product by tracking it from the certified source through the chain of custody, in order to guarantee that it comes from a certified source. Following certification assessment, a certification seal or label is often attached to the firm or product so that consumers can readily identify it as being certified (Poncibò, 2007).

Environmental and social labelling schemes go back to the 1970s but have multiplied since the 1990s. How many schemes are in operation today throughout OECD is not known. As of April 2006, the US Consumer Union listed on its website 137 eco-labels found in the US market alone for the following standards: organic, pest management, social responsibility, no genetic engineering, sustainable agriculture, sustainable fishing, animal welfare, sustainable wood and general claims. Most social labels that we know of today came into existence in the 1990s. Unlike for eco-labels, no national or regional initiatives have been developed. Whereas environmental standards can relate to either production methods which leave a trace in the final product (e.g. cotton grown using pesticides whose residues remain in the cotton itself) or product-unrelated production methods leaving no trace in the final product (e.g. steel produced at different emission levels), social labels convey information of the latter type. Drawing on Simon Zadek *et al.* (1998), social labels can be self-declared (e.g. Tea Corporate Brands), developed by industry bodies (e.g. GlobalGAP) or by partnerships (e.g. Forest Stewardship Council), NGO-led (e.g. Fair Trade mark) or sponsored by governments (e.g. Kaleen).

The main strengths of labelling schemes as an information tool are their visibility at point of purchase as well as their simplicity. Labels help consumers to clearly identify and select a product. Labels can appeal especially to consumers that have no time to search for information about the attributes of goods and services that are not readily visible. From a more general perspective, eco-labels remain one of the most widely accepted ways for a company to communicate environmental credentials (UNEP, 2005). Certification carried out by an independent third party give labels credibility, and some have achieved a high level of trust and recognition internationally. All in all, the number of companies/licences which have joined national eco-label initiatives to date indicates that a growing number of companies are willing to take advantage of labelling schemes to provide product information for consumers.

*Eco-labels remain one of the most widely accepted ways for a company to communicate environmental credentials*

Labelling schemes as information tools also have some weaknesses. First and foremost, they are not easily adopted for intermediate goods. Labels furthermore presuppose that consumers know the underlying criteria, i.e. what a label stands for. Often this is not the case. For example, some consumers buy premium-priced 'free-range' eggs not because they care about animal welfare but because they think that these eggs are really fresh (Miele and Parisi, 1998). This lack of knowledge is compounded by an apparent multiplication of labelling schemes based on more or less similar standards, which confuses consumers and causes them to avoid the products altogether. Consumers do not have the time to research what the criteria for a label are, and how the criteria of different labels compare.

When studying the coffee market, Daniele Giovannucci (2003) found that consumer confusion was indeed a problem, especially in European markets featuring a large number of labelling schemes and similar initiatives. This is not only a problem for consumers but also for producers who are paying for certification in the hope to sustain and expand their sales. Experience over time with eco-labelling also shows that labelling can be subject to misrepresentation. However, the success of labelling schemes appears to depend critically on consumers being aware of and being able to understand such schemes. Education remains a challenge for the operators of such schemes (and governments) as well as clearer labelling in order to satisfy the consumers' desire to judge properly whether or not products meet CSR production criteria.

## Informing consumers: corporate marketing

CSR information can also reach consumers through the channels of corporate marketing and advertising. Companies can use traditional marketing tools, like advertising, PR campaigns, cause-related marketing on the one hand, or non-traditional marketing tools, like off-media communication and Web-based marketing on the other. What channel, or what tools, they use for their marketing mix depends on their overall strategy, the positioning of their product or the sector they operate in.

Packaging is also an important part of visual marketing. It can convey a message about a particular brand, a producer's CSR stance, the naturalness or environmental friendliness of the product and the package is also a medium to display self-declared CSR labels or awards earned by the product. An important factor determining the credibility of CSR-related claims on product packaging may be how specific the claims are. It has been found that when general packaging claims ('ozone friendly') were coupled with specific qualifiers ('no CFCs') this led consumers to perceive a product as safer for the environment than when either only a general claim or only a specific claim was presented (Maronick and Andrews, 1999). While general claims may be perceived as obscure because they cannot be verified, specific claims may be hard to interpret on their own. When used together, they may compensate each other's weaknesses and increase consumer trust.

*Advertising and product packaging appear to be quite adequate in establishing CSR as a credible product attribute in consumers' eyes*

Next to the well-known use of the package as an information channel, companies also use less conventional marketing tools. Often a salient characteristic of these new tools is that they try to market a brand or product without being perceived as doing so by the consumer (e.g. through sponsoring, conference participation or organising, printing and distributing CSR-related brochures, street communication, Web-based forums and bulletin boards). This can be explained by the fact that overt advertisement of a company is usually perceived by consumers as a less trustworthy source, and leaves the consumer feeling sceptical about a brand. Moreover, advertising CSR overtly is risky. To build publicity on CSR can confuse consumers about the message of the advertiser or render them distrustful. Companies can do more damage than good by merely stating their environmental or social commitments because many people do not trust advertising claims.

Reviewing a large body of studies investigating the effectiveness of CSR communication, Guido Berens (2006) concludes that corporate communication through advertising and product packaging appear to be quite adequate in establishing CSR as a credible product attribute in consumers' eyes.

Another way to inform consumers is to publish magazines for consumers to inform them about a company's brands, communication schemes (environmental sponsoring, or NGO partnership of a brand, for instance), or newly published CSR reports. As a general rule though, only big corporations can afford these expensive full-colour, multiple page printouts. Since they have many different brands, some meeting CSR standards and others not or not entirely, CSR issues remain pretty rare in those magazines, and they are not the media of choice for brands to communicate their CSR stance.

Providing evidence of internal alignment through a mix of non-financial reporting, public relations, awareness campaigns, rather than relying mostly on corporate communication and advertising, will help build consumers' trust. Materialising evidence, through products and connection to consumers' lives, as well as making the reporting transparent to prevent 'greenwashing' suspicion are important to maintain this trust.

Companies sometimes include other stakeholders in their communication policies. For example, they might partner with NGOs, which can enhance their reputation or provide specialised expertise that they do not have. Also, employees can be a company's ambassadors in terms of conveying the CSR message of a company and its brands. Employee blogs, for instance, to which consumers can turn for information about a company's practices, production and product information, have helped enhance the reputation of their employers (e.g. Stonefield Farms, Microsoft, Sun Microsystem) or damaged it (e.g. Google, Delta Air Lines, or Friendster). Blogs influence news, analysts, and regulators. These new forms of internal and external communication are not to be underestimated.

## Informing consumers: other channels

Information can reach consumers in multiple ways. Corporate CSR reports and consumer guides are other instruments that supply information about CSR to markets.

To begin with, some attention is paid to corporate CSR reports. Responding to the increasing demand for disclosure of their social and environmental performance, a growing number of companies annually or periodically publish reports describing activities related to CSR, which are also accessible on their websites in varying formats. 52% of the top half of Fortune 500 corporations and 33% of the top 100 companies in 16 countries issued separate CSR reports in 2005. The CSR Network 2003 Benchmark Survey Report corroborated these findings, including huge differences from industry to industry (led by financial services, electronics and automotives) and geography to geography (led by Japan, the United Kingdom and Canada) (KPMG 2005). Today's corporate reports cover a wide range of issues on the CSR agenda. A clear tendency is that environmental reporting has broadened to include social and sometimes also financial issues. The development of guidelines or standards relating to procedure and contents of reporting or other forms of corporate communication with various stakeholders are leading to increasingly streamlined reporting, measuring and auditing standards that reflect real-life situations rather than merely aspirational goals.

Compared to labels and other information schemes, corporate reports provide more detailed information, and some consumers indeed appear familiar with corporate reports. For example, about half of the respondents from North America, Australia and some parts of Europe participating in a recent survey stated that they had either read or at least briefly looked at a CSR report themselves, or heard about one from somebody else (GlobeScan, 2005). However, companies do not prepare their reports with consumers in mind, and the information disclosed is often complex and usually geared towards presenting a company's overall performance, not the attributes of its individual lines of products. Reporting criteria and standards also vary across companies, making it difficult for the average consumer to compare companies. Finally, while going public through the incorporation of a CSR report within the company's annual report increases CSR awareness and helps communication with external stakeholders, passive reporting is not enough and needs to be complemented by proactive publicity if the goal is to build a reservoir of social goodwill towards a specific company and its products (Werther and Chandler, 2005).

Secondly, buying guides published by consumer organisations or other public and private entities are better targeted at consumers. Thousands of consumer guides offer product information, including prices, specifications, features, reviews, results of testing and comparisons. The likes of *Consumer Reports* and *BestBuy* in the United States or *60 Millions de Consommateurs* in France have accumulated a stock of trust with the general public that is perceived as a natural counterweight to the overwhelming presence of corporate advertising. More recently, buying guides and consumer information magazines began to cover CSR issues, ranking companies or making product recommendations based on environmental, social, fair trade or ethical considerations. These include *Ethical Consumer* and *newconsumer* in the United Kingdom, *GreenerChoices* and *BuildingGreen* in the United States and *Consumer* in New Zealand, whose declared objective is to promote universal human rights and environmental sustainability through ethical purchasing. They usually give detailed information about the producer's environmental reporting, sustainable farming, forced and child labour record, its code of conduct, irresponsible marketing, genetic engineering, and the like, further supplying references to specialised watchdogs like *Corporate Critic, Fair Trade Foundation* and *Anti-Slavery International* in the United Kingdom, *Corporate Europe Observatory* in the Netherlands or *CorpWatch* in the United States. Experimental studies confirm the consumer guides' potential for influencing consumer attitudes and purchasing preferences when information is provided on environmental or labour conditions of production (see Mohr and Webb, 2005; Swaen and Vanhamme, 2005). It is not clear whether buying guides and consumer information magazines are of more negative than positive use to consumers, that is, to what extent they serve as catalysts for boycotts rather than buying trends. What is clear is that consumers respond well to information on CSR when it is offered in a systematic and comparable way. Consumer guides are at the frontline of such efforts and have a reputation for being impartial and trustworthy. This is important enough because consumers' confidence in the message and trust in the messenger are central to whether the information supplied has an impact on consumer attitudes and purchasing behaviour.

## CSR communication in the fish market

After having explored a range of communication tools through which consumers are informed about the social and environmental conditions of production, we now turn to a description of the state of play of CSR communication in the current food economy. This section concentrates on the fish market, while the following section focuses on the market of cut flowers.

The fish sector is under pressure. An estimated quarter of fish stocks are already overexploited or depleted and around half of stocks have reached their maximum level of exploitation. Not surprisingly perhaps, aside from health and safety issues, key concerns arising in the fisheries have to do with the management of a resource and associated environmental issues, and more specifically 'sustainable fisheries'. Working conditions have figured less prominently, although fishermen work in a dangerous environment and occupational fatalities far exceed national averages in many countries. Another feature of this market is that the once relatively short fishery supply chain – with fishermen and local fishmongers selling directly to consumers – has given way to a global network of fishing vessels and aquaculture establishments, processors, wholesalers and retailers, with supermarket chains today supplying a large share of seafood bought by consumers. This transformation has removed fish as a product many steps away from the end consumer, leaving him unfamiliar with how fish is caught, how it impacts on

*Consumers respond well to information on CSR when it is offered in a systematic and comparable way*

the ecosystem and why movement towards sustainable production is necessary.

Most fishing enterprises communicate their commitment to principles of sustainable fishing to consumers and other stakeholders through labelling, websites, company reports or other modes. However, information gaps still exist, making it difficult for consumers to, for example, identify types of seafood that are overfished or caught in ways harmful to other sea creatures and the ocean environment. Certification and eco-labelling is the most widely employed CSR information tool. Centring on consumer interest in food quality and safety but also growing interest in purchasing products that have been sustainably harvested, quite a number of national or global programmes have emerged during the last decade, prompting the FAO Committee of Fisheries to adopt a set of voluntary Guidelines for the Ecolabelling of Fish Products in 2005.

Many labelling schemes have gained widespread recognition. One was developed by the Marine Stewardship Council (MSC) and provides labelling services for fish and seafood originating from marines catches separately in two stages – the fish harvesting and the downstream supply chain. Fisheries from a variety of jurisdictions and scales are entering the MSC certification process, as are the stakeholders from the entire production chain. As a result, in ten years the label has grown to cover 300 fish products in 25 countries around the world. Retail sales of MSC-labelled seafood jumped 76% from 2005 to 2006, and the number of seafood products carrying the label rose 50%. For some fish the label is already very important: 42% of the world's wild salmon fisheries, and 32% of prime whitefish fisheries are MSC-certified.

In the Asia-Pacific region, in view of increasing demand for and trade in live reef food fish (LRFF) and the resulting overexploitation and use of destructive fishing practices a voluntary industry-level LRFF Standard finalised in 2004 covers the entire chain of custody and trading – capture, handling, holding distribution and marketing of reef food fish. The standard does not involve certification and labelling, considered inappropriate because of the large volumes and number of species traded, the diffuse nature of the industry and the unique 'live' aspect of the product (Muldoon and Scott, 2005). Nonetheless, low awareness among Asian consumers of sustainability issues involving live food fish, and their declared preference for wild caught over aquaculture live reef fish, has caused a discount price for aquaculture fish and provided little incentive for scaling back catches of wild LRFF and developing sustainable aquaculture techniques. Implementation of another live reef fisheries programme which involves third-party certification and a label – that of the Marine Aquarium Council (MAC) targeting sustainability of the collection of wild ornamental aquarium fish and coral reef ecosystems – appears to be faring better.

*Dolphin-safe labels are a typical case where numerous labels compete with each other in the market place – perhaps resulting in too much choice so that consumers are confused*

'Dolphin-safe' or 'Dolphin-friendly' labels applied to tuna products are another group of better-known eco-labels. There are several third-party schemes as well as a large number of self-declared dolphin-safe labels: the three largest US tuna processors, namely Starkist, Bumble Bee tuna, and Chicken of the Sea all have their own dolphin-safe logos. Dolphin-safe labels are a typical case where numerous labels compete with each other in the market place – perhaps resulting in too much choice so that consumers are confused.

While retail sales of fish products carrying an eco-label account for less than 1% of the total seafood market, interest in certified fish on the part of consumers and retailers around the world is increasing. At the retail level, big supermarket chains prefer to deal with certified seafood, but the nature of fisheries is such that labelling is difficult to undertake, particularly in terms of verifying and monitoring, because most fishing takes place in remote seas and requires further processing. Unless handled separately, fish from different sources may be mixed during processing. Hence some observers question the integrity of fish labels, and fishery labels are still struggling to gain and sustain credibility among consumers and producers. Nonetheless, sustainable management certification is supported by growing demand for it, including from food service retailers such as McDonald's, Darden Restaurants and Bon Appetit Management Company.

As far as corporate advertising and marketing is concerned, many fish harvesting and processing companies as well as seafood retailers provide information and communicate with consumers and other stakeholders via their homepages on the Internet. On their websites, many fisheries companies state their commitments to sustainable fishing and provide related information. Another way of informing consumers is through product packaging (using such terms as natural, eco, fresh, bio, organic and pure or use self-declared labels as in the case of private dolphin-safe tuna labels). Corporate reporting is not widely used. Unilever and Sanford Ltd are exceptions to the rule that companies from fisheries do not publish stand-alone CSR reports. Fish and fish products are also hard to find in consumer guides. These guides do not usually include product recommendations for seafood and, if any, they provide quality-related but not environmental and social information. Recently some environmental organisations, semi-state agencies and NGOs (e.g. Marine Conservation Society in UK, Forest & Bird in New Zealand, Seafood Choices Alliance and Audubon Society in USA) have begun to publish fish guides. Typically these locally-oriented guides list fish species that are recommended or to be avoided, together with information on fishing gear, catch methods, by-catch and biology. They usually use a traffic-light approach and sometimes issue handy guides in pocket or wallet format for consultation when shopping or in restaurants. These fish guides do not identify specific producers, processors and suppliers.

## CSR communication in the market of cut flowers

The advantage of growing low-priced mass-produced cut flowers has shifted over the last ten to fifteen years away from the OECD region to Colombia, Kenya and other developing countries with a favourable growing climate and low production costs. Meanwhile, consumption remains concentrated in Western Europe, North America and Japan. The auction houses in the Netherlands remain the leading market outlet for flowers worldwide, but wholesalers and supermarket chains are procuring growing volumes of flowers also directly from growers or their import agents. Production practices in this industry have attracted media coverage and public attention since the early 1990s, when campaigns by labour unions, environmental groups and other NGOs took issue with the poor working conditions, unsafe use of pesticides and other toxic substances on African and Latin American flower farms.

Labelling programmes telling end consumers whether flower growing farms adhere to some standard covering environmental and labour conditions, are still relatively rare. Information schemes used are dominated by buyer or industry codes of conduct covering worker health and safety, employment conditions and/or environmental performance. Examples are the Dutch Milieu Programma Sierteelt, the Florverde label in Colombia, Sello Verde in Ecuador, and the Kenya Flower Council's code of practice. These schemes may involve labels or symbols attesting conformance to these standards, but they are meant to facilitate business-to-business transactions along supply chains. Their standard is often the International Code of Conduct for the Production of Cut Flowers (ICC), developed in 1998 by the European flower campaign with the participation of NGOs and labour unions. ICC builds on international human rights standards, basic environmental standards and ILO Conventions and has been accepted by many flower distributors, especially in Europe. The associated labels are increasingly recognised in the international floricultural trade, with wholesale buyers often aware of them. Activity at this level has been intensive. For instance, with social and environmental code compliance being encouraged by European buyers, Kenya reportedly has one of the most codified flower industries in the world (Collinson, 2001).

*Labelling programmes telling end consumers whether flower growing farms adhere to some standard covering environmental and labour conditions, are still relatively rare*

Consumer labels are mostly found in the European market. Besides programmes like Fair Trade Certified, the German Flower Label Programme, and the Fair Flowers and Plants (FFP) label launched in 2005 by the International Flower Trade Association, cut flowers have recently found their way into the Fair Trade Certified schemes of European countries such as the UK, Switzerland, Belgium, and Norway. There are 20 national labelling initiatives across Europe, North America and Japan – known under such different labels as Max Havelaar, TransFair, and Fairtrade – which license the Fair Trade label in their respective countries. These labels tell consumers that producers receive a guaranteed fair price and that their purchases make a contribution towards helping primary producers and their workers overcome economic marginalisation. Unlike Fair Trade Certified, the Flower Label Programme (FLP) applies exclusively to cut flowers and targets growers in developing countries exporting to the German market. FLP-certified flower farms commit to environmental and social standards based on the ICC standard and are publicly known. Shoppers can look up German florists participating in the programme by consulting a database on the Internet. Similarly, the Fair Flowers and Plants (FFP) label introduced by the International Flower Trade Association in 2005 makes available electronic databases giving contact details for florists, wholesalers and even participating flower farms. In North America and elsewhere, certification and labelling schemes have taken hold only recently (for example, the Sierra Eco label in Canada, and the VeraFlora Certified Sustainably Grown label, under which several US and Latin American producers have been certified).

*As a general rule, it is not possible to trace flowers bought from a florist shop, back to a specific flower grower*

As yet, in the cut flower market, production conditions and other CSR issues are not usually addressed through overt marketing and advertising. Some online shops specialise in selling cut flowers that are certified, but large wire or web-based flower order services operating in the OECD region advertise that they carry such certified products. At times, information on production practices can be found on websites that individual flower farms themselves have created, but as a general rule it is not possible to trace flowers bought from a florist shop back to a specific flower grower.

In the fledgling niche market of organically grown cut flowers, the industry of some OECD countries is visibly engaged in creating public awareness, educating consumers and positioning company brands. Flowers that are grown organically are eligible for inclusion in some of the existing voluntary organic certification programmes for agricultural produce, and can fetch a premium when marketed as upscale products although not all cut flower producers believe organic growing can be profitable. New labels are emerging for this niche of the cut flower market, a development which is not confined to Europe but is also taking hold in the flower trade in North America.

With rare exceptions such as Dole Food Company Inc., corporate reporting providing information about floricultural production conditions is not a standard practice of growers, retailers or supermarkets. Similarly, consumers consulting guides on consumer goods will seldom come across CSR information for cut flowers. Neither do the consumer-oriented informative websites on floriculture mention flower certification labels or CSR in the flower industry. For the interested shopper the websites or electronic newsletters of civil society groups engaged in this industry (e.g. Flower Coordination Switzerland, Fairtrade Foundation in UK, and International Labour Rights Fund in the USA) are possibly the most readily accessible sources of information.

## Fish, flowers and the future of CSR

Certification and label programmes dominate other communication strategies in the markets for fish and flowers. In both sectors business-to-business programmes aim at ensuring and tracing adherence to CSR standards by parties within the supply chain. As a result, products that meet responsible production standards are not necessarily identified as such to consumers at the point of purchase. The fact that CSR consumer labelling is not yet as developed as in some other consumer goods markets may have something to do with the commodity-type nature of fish and cut flowers. Most fishing takes place in remote seas and fish from different sources can be mixed during processing, irrespective of their harvesting method. Similarly, selling certified and uncertified flowers at the same retail outlet raises issues such as how to handle mixed bouquets and how to monitor compliance of the many outlets that sell flowers. Besides, in the fish and seafood industry CSR has taken root only recently. The market for fish from sustainably managed fisheries is small, but national as well as international schemes for certifying and promoting labels for fish and fisheries products from well-managed marine captured fisheries are gaining ground, driven by consumer demand as well as by companies' desire to remain in business in an increasingly fragile resource sector. More direct relations between producers and retailers, observed in floriculture where large retail companies and supermarkets increasingly source directly from growers or their export agents, could reduce the investment needed to supply consumer information while making CSR performance more transparent (OECD, 2006).

*The future of CSR with respect to foods, fish or flowers, will depend on a carefully chosen mix of mass advertising and non-traditional marketing channels and extensive use of the media to convey to customers their CSR image*

It accounts for both fish and flowers that brand identity is weak. There are few if any specialised producers or retailers with brand names that the general public instantly recognise. CSR reporting is not widespread. Advertising and other forms of marketing to inform consumers of companies' CSR performance is relatively limited and far from matching the product positioning that exists for many other consumer products. A good case is cosmetics, where companies like Natura, The Body Shop and Aveda have branded their products around CSR, making environmental and social standards of production an integral part of the brand and image of the company.

The agro-food complex in general, and the fish and cut flowers sectors in particular, have a long way to go before reaching this position. In comparison to other consumer goods information about foods, fish products or flowers that meet CSR standards is often not readily available and you need to be a motivated consumer to find it. The future of CSR with respect to foods, fish or flowers, will therefore depend on a carefully chosen mix of mass advertising and non-traditional marketing channels and extensive use of the media to convey to customers their CSR image in terms of employee treatment and involvement, animal testing, biodiversity, human rights, resource consumption and waste management, partnerships with NGOs, and ingredients. The importance and impact of CSR will increase when general or specialised consumer guides carry more information about conditions of production and other CSR issues with respect to agro-food products, such as consumer safety issues (e.g. pesticides, chemical ingredients). As CSR products are being streamlined into the mass market, result-focused communication – i.e. providing consumers with factual information about the impact at production level – might become the next frontier for competitive product differentiation and company branding. Last but not least, the future of CSR will be brighter as long as producers and buyers operating in the agro-food sector incorporate CSR standards into their competitive strategies for product differentiation and consumer communication strategies.

# The interplay between private and public food safety standards

*Pepijn van de Port*

Food chain operators all across the globe are 'confronted' with standards relating to food safety. Part of them will be imposed on them by their clients, others will be imposed on them by their governments. Some of them will be a requisite for operating their business, others will be a condition for obtaining an export license or export certificate or for a specific sale, and are thus part of the contract. Some have to be applied for at government agencies, others have 'to be bought' at international certifying companies like SGS international or the Aquaculture Certification Council. This new prominence of standards in global agro-trade might be seen as a new global food safety regime. A regime distinguished from its forebears by two novelties. Firstly, it is characterised by a shift away from product quality controls in favor of controls on food operator processes and management. Quality Assurance Schemes like Hazard Analysis and Critical Control Points (HACCP) or ISO 9000 are increasingly made mandatory for food chain operators all over the world. Secondly, the new regime is characterised by a fading distinction between the private and public spheres. Where the government once claimed all responsibility for food safety in its territory, food safety assurance is now sought by a complex interplay between public and private actors.

## Protection of public health

This latter trend recently provoked a lot of discussion in the WTO Committee on Sanitary and Phytosanitary Measures (SPS). Although the stated goal of all these HACCP-based standards is to promote public health and to facilitate international trade, according to the Codex Alimentarius Commission, they were also increasingly perceived as trade barriers. They therefore became an issue in the WTO Uruguay round of negotiations on agriculture. It resulted in an agreement on 'the Application of Sanitary and Phytosanitary Measures'. In essence, this agreement allows importing states to set minimum requirements for imported foodstuffs at the level of the international food safety standards issued by the Codex Commission. It only allows higher levels of protection of public health when backed by convincing scientific evidence that the risks really exist, and, it explicitly demands importing states to accept different ways to achieve the required outcomes. States are not allowed to prescribe a certain way of production, but have to limit themselves to characteristics of the product. Lastly, the WTO being an organisation of states, the SPS agreement by definition only covers standards set by public bodies (Barton *et al.*, 2006).

More or less to the surprise of the importing nations, developing nations still felt they were confronted with technical trade barriers revolving around the issue of protection of public health. This time however, these trade barriers were not embodied in public standards but in private standards. When asked, however, importing food chain operators stated that these standards were forced upon them by their domestic national authorities. First Uruguay, and later St. Vincent and the Grenadines, brought the issue before the SPS committee, claiming that these private standards in fact are public standards in disguise. Initially the SPS-committee reacted in a formal way, refusing to address the issue because it was outside their scope. When the discussion persisted, the SPS secretariat inquired among its member-nations if the issue should be addressed, stating that they themselves felt that indeed 'the division of public and private standards had become blurry' (WTO, 2007).

*States are not allowed to prescribe a certain way of production, but have to limit themselves to characteristics of the product*

## Public and private intertwined

New as this 'blurring' of public and private spheres of standards might seem from the legalistic view of the WTO agreement, in fact there has never been a strict distinction between the two. Many private standards developed by the industry in time became public standards. Public standards often were an answer on private standards, but when these public standards obtained a firm footing, trade or industry organisations tended to orient their new private standards on these public standards (Cheit, 1990; Porter and Ronit, 2006). And public and private standards also interact in another way. Experts of (parts of ) the industry play a substantial role in the technical committees that are preparing new international or national standards (Brunsson *et al.*, 2002; Hallstrom, 2004). On the other side, many private standards are written by organisations like the 'American Conference of Government Industrial Hygienists', the 'Association of Official Agricultural Chemists' or the 'Society of Public Analysts', all important private standards setters, but at the same time organisations of professionals employed as public servants (Cheit, 1990; Smith and Phillips, 2000). As a result, although developed by different actors, for the use by different organisations, and on behalf of very different recipients, the actual content of public and private standards appear very much alike. They all refer to the same notions and principles, and, to make things even more complex, they increasingly start to refer to each other. The development and setting of both public and private standards in practice thus has always been somewhat of a joint venture of both public and private parties. What needs to be explained with respect to the sudden proliferation of private standards in international trade of agricultural products is therefore not so much the sudden entrance of private standards in the global trading regime. The question should rather be what exactly has changed in the international agro-trade regime to make the underlying blurred and intertwined practices of public and private standard setters become so apparent.

*The actual content of public and private standards appear very much alike; they all refer to the same notions and principles*

## HACCP as due diligence defense

The new food and feed-safety legislation in the EU is based on two premises. The first basic premise states that establishments within the food and feed production chain themselves have to be responsible for the quality of their product (EU/DG SANCO, 2006). As a consequence, food safety authorities no longer assume responsibility for the safety of food, but have redefined their role as public policing of the (now mandatory) policing of food safety by operators in the food chain. Of course, this newly imposed responsibility of the operators in the feed and food chain came with a stick to force them into action. European law on feed (regulation 183 (2005) art.8.1) explicitly calls for the transposition of this new responsibility into the financial liability for 'the total costs for which operators could be held liable as a direct consequence of the withdrawal from the market, treatment and/or destruction of any feed, animals and food produced therefrom'.

Surprisingly, and contrary to common opinion, as of yet there is no European legislation providing for liability for food chain operators. If provided for at all, liability for food operators is provided for by national legislation only (EU, 2007). Notwithstanding this, the great majority of food operators feel that because they are made responsible by EU regulation, they are at risk of being held liable by customers and by the state. Operators, of course, are looking for ways to diminish their vulnerability in court. Liability, due diligence, and negligence are legal notions that originate from the Anglo-Saxon common law tradition. Common law demands that a person takes 'reasonable' precautions to avoid harm to another party: due diligence. If, and only if he fails to do so, a person is liable for the damages his actions caused. The question then becomes what can be considered a 'reasonable precaution'. It is here that the second premise in the EU food regulation kicks in. For it states that food and feed quality is best assured by the implementation of a HACCP-based quality assurance approach. By doing so, EU food safety regulation thus defines for feed and food chain operators that implementation of HACCP-based quality assurance will suffice as a valid 'due diligence' defense.

HACCP is not a new approach to quality assurance (Hulebak and Schlosser, 2002). It originates from the late 1960s, and in essence is an attempt to define and then prevent the occurrence of food hazards by systematically eliminating all vectors of hazardous contamination. Part of these vectors can be eliminated by interventions in the production process. Microbiological hazards for example can be controlled by chilling, cooking or cleaning. Other vectors can only be eliminated by a strict control on inputs. Residues of agro-chemicals for example can be controlled by extensive testing of all material inputs like supplied raw materials or water. Central to HACCP is the methodical approach. All identified vectors at all possible stages of production need to be addressed systematically and then handled according to a master plan. The proper working of that master plan needs to be monitored continually, and evaluated periodically, both internally as well as by external parties.

What is prescribed in EU regulations, then, is not so much a technical, but a managerial approach, in which the assurances for quality are sought for in controls of records of test results and work sheets listing performed activities. Much of HACCP relies on prudent record keeping. This managerial angle in HACCP has some distinct advantages. Assuming that test results are recorded faithfully and worksheets are filled in truthfully, it allows for strict managerial control of the processes within the establishment. It also allows for efficient state controls of the establishment, and likewise allows for efficient third party control. But most importantly, the managerial approach in HACCP makes it possible to replace costly and time-consuming laboratory testing of supplied inputs with administrative controls on the quality assurances of the supplier.

*What is prescribed in EU regulations, then, is not so much a technical, but a managerial approach*

This latter kind of control means that the buyer needs to check on the quality assurance systems of the supplier. It might do so itself, but usually the buyer makes certification against the backdrop of a HACCP-based food safety standard a precondition for supplying. Requiring one's supplier to be certified against a HACCP standard of the supplier thus serves the due diligence defense of the buyer. And indeed, private standard setters like the British Retail Consortium (BRC) or the

SQF Institute market their standards by emphasising that sourcing from a certified supplier will serve as a 'due diligence defence' in a liability suit. And, of course, there are a number of other good reasons to ask for certification. Retailers especially need to defend their good name, and in some cases (e.g. BRC) standards are so publicly known that they also serve marketing ends. But in general, and especially in the sphere of business-to-business interaction, the (announced) new EU regulations drove food chain operators into attempts to cover for liability by asking their suppliers to certify against HACCP standards.

## Public food safety controls

Having placed the final responsibility with the food chain operator and having forced HACCP on food and feed operations, EU regulations are starting to develop into a regulatory system of public food safety controls. The way these regulations are stated, however, reinforce the private control regime the EU imposed on food chain operators. Member states of the EU have to ensure the EU-wide implementation of this approach by making registration of food processing establishments mandatory, and subsequently by making the implementation of HACCP-based controls a precondition for registration. It means that although *working* according to a HACCP-based quality assurance plan is considered to be a private responsibility, *having* such a plan in place is made mandatory by the state. Only primary producers (farmers, fishers, gatherers and hunters) are excluded from these requirements. Next to this, the EU insists on having traceability in place: a paper trail via which food (components) can be traced back to the farm/field/pond from which they originated. Again, it is a 'public' requirement that greatly facilitates the 'private' use of certification as a control on supplied inputs. Lastly, it provides for an inspection system that via sampling monitors the effectiveness of both the individual operator-controls and the public controls on the food and feed chain as a whole (EU, 2002).

*Working according to a HACCP-based quality assurance plan is considered to be a private responsibility, having such a plan in place is made mandatory by the state*

Apart from these three systems (registration, traceability and product testing) focusing directly on the feed and food chain and its operators, there is a whole complex of additional measures in place in the EU to ensure that harmful substances or agents will not enter the food chain. Standards exist for the quality of water sources, surrounding surface waters and effluents, and these are monitored by state agencies. Agro-chemicals like fertilizers, pesticides and animal medicines need to be approved and registered before they can be sold. Animal medicines are available only on prescription, and have to be issued by a registered veterinarian. Additionally a public health system is in place for monitoring and controlling the occurrence of contagious diseases, both veterinary and human. Although these measures and controls are not directly connected to the food and feed chain, indirectly they do serve the purpose of food safety within the chain because they greatly diminish the number of potential hazardous vectors that have to be taken into account within the HACCP analysis. It is these state controls on the direct environment of the farm that allow for the exemption of the primary producer (the farm) from the obligation to have HACCP-based plans and controls in place. Within the EU the primary producer is – by regulation – required to comply with state imposed 'measures to control contamination arising from the air, soil, water, feed, fertilisers, veterinary medicinal products, plant protection products and biocides and the storage, handling and disposal of waste' (EU, 2004). The primary producer in effect has to work according to Good Agricultural Practices, must instantly comply with any measures the state wants to impose upon him, but is not burdened with a mandatory HACCP approach. The primary producer, in other words, is allowed to rely on the state's monitoring and safeguarding the quality of its inputs like soil, water or veterinary services.

## Food safety controls on imports

Having arranged the food safety of domestic produce, the EU then turned its attention to the food safety of imported food stuffs. And once again the cornerstone of the EU regulatory approach is to put the responsibility with the importing food business operator by stating that 'it is incumbent upon the importer to ensure compliance with the relevant requirements of food law or with conditions recognised equivalent hereto by the community' (EU/DG SANCO, 2006). How importers have to ensure this compliance is nowhere defined or suggested in EU regulations, but it will be no surprise to learn that most importers simply applied the strategy they already used within the EU to ward off liability. So, en masse, they started asking their foreign suppliers to certify based on HACCP food safety standards like SQF 1000/2000 or GlobalGAP. Such certification meant that also the up-stream suppliers of these exporters had to have HACCP-based quality assurance plans and controls in place. In effect, all foreign elements of the supply chain into the EU had to be organised according to HACCP principles – but this time they included the primary producers as well.

*The success of the new EU food safety policy relies heavily on isolating exporting parts of the foreign food chain from its environment with HACCP-based instruments*

It is precisely the latter that the EU itself cannot demand. The EU has to comply with the WTO and SPS agreements. In the case of imports the SPS agreement and Codex regulations entitle the EU to ask for equivalence only. As in the EU, foreign primary producers should be exempted from mandatory HACCP plans and controls, and should be allowed to rely on state monitoring and safeguarding of their inputs. At the same time it is clear that the kind of food safety the EU is trying to establish can only be guaranteed when the (controls on the) environment of the foreign farm are EU-equivalent, or alternatively, the inputs and processes at the level of the farm are monitored in a strict, HACCP-based manner. Given the fact that a true equivalence for developing countries is a sheer impossibility, the success of the new EU food safety policy relies heavily on isolating exporting parts of the foreign food chain from its environment with HACCP-based instruments. And that is exactly the approach the EU guidelines on food imports seem to promote.

Recently published leaflets and guidance documents on changes in the EU food safety approach always stress that for foreign exporting operators and exporting nations nothing or very little will change in reality. That might be true in a formal sense. But at the core of the new EU food safety approach lies the dynamic that a state forces its domestic operators to impose a certain method of quality assurance upon its foreign primary producers that the state itself cannot ask for. It might be what is needed to protect the public health of EU citizens. But it is most definitely a 'public' use of private standards.

# Making the livestock sector more sustainable[4]

*Henning Steinfeld*

The livestock sector is a major stressor on many ecosystems. Simultaneously, we rate environmental considerations as important. Public awareness is growing worldwide that there are boundaries to the world's natural resources. Finite, non-replenishable natural resources such as fossil fuels rapidly dwindle due to human activities and even replenishable natural resources such as fish populations are threatened in their existence. This 'inconvenient truth' becomes more evident with a growing and wealthier world population. The damage inflicted by livestock production leaves future generations with a debt. Environmental costs created by some groups and nations are carried by others, or by the planet as a whole. The health of the environment and the availability of resources affect the welfare of future generations, and overuse of resources and excess environmental pollution by current generations are to their detriment.

## Livestock sector and sustainability

It is within this context not merely for academic reasons interesting to examine the livestock sector's responsibility for a significant share of environmental change but also for additional reasons of social and political urgency. Sustainability is among the top issues at the agenda of both public administrations and private boards. In order to achieve sustainability, public administrations finally develop and implement more stringent policies and build and extend supporting institutions. At the same time as governments sharpen environmental policies, private companies take up their own responsibility by developing corporate social responsibility policies. Sustainable livestock production is not only vital to the environmental health of the world

---

[4] This chapter is a revised version of the executive summary of *Livestock's Long Shadow* (2006).

as a whole, but also to the economic vitality and public acceptability of the livestock sector itself. Thus, both for the sake of the sector and for helping to save the world, there is need for the livestock sector to change into more sustainable directions. The livestock production should avoid to be equated with an environmental threat through reversing the trend of an ever increasing environmental impact.

Making livestock production more sustainable is not going to be an easy job. First, because there is a lack of understanding about the nature and extent of livestock's impact on the environment. The understanding of livestock-environment interactions is poor, because they involve many complex and indirect relations. Second, because current policy frameworks are either non-existent or rudimentary at best. Environmental policies are either non-existent or poorly implemented in developing countries, certainly in remote areas. In developed countries, livestock producers still wield large political influence and are able to block environmental policies.

This chapter deals with the impact of the livestock sector on environmental problems. This is important enough as the livestock sector is one of the top two or three most significant contributors to the most serious environmental problems, at every scale from local to global. Livestock's contribution to environmental problems is on a massive scale and its potential contribution to their solution is equally large. The impact is so significant that it needs to be addressed with urgency. For this reason, this chapter suggests that it should be a major policy focus when dealing with problems of land degradation, climate change and air pollution, water shortage and water pollution and loss of biodiversity.

## Importance and impact of the sector

Although economically not a major global player – it generates about 1.4% of the world's gross domestic product (GDP) – the livestock sector is socially and politically very significant. It accounts for 40% of agricultural GDP. It employs 1.3 billion people and creates livelihoods for one billion of the world's poor. Livestock products provide one-third of humanity's protein intake, and are a contributing cause of obesity and a potential remedy for undernourishment.

Growing populations and incomes, along with changing food preferences, are rapidly increasing demand for livestock products, while globalisation is boosting trade in livestock inputs and products. Global production of meat is projected to more than double from 229 million tonnes in 1999/01 to 465 million tonnes in 2050, and that of milk to grow from 580 to 1043 million tonnes. The environmental impact per unit of livestock production must be cut by half, just to avoid the level of damage worsening beyond its present level.

At present, the livestock sector is undergoing a complex process of technical and geographical change, which is shifting the balance of environmental problems caused by the sector. Extensive grazing still occupies and degrades vast areas of land; though there is an increasing trend towards intensification and industrialisation. Livestock production is shifting geographically, first from rural areas to urban and peri-urban, to get closer to consumers, then towards the sources of feedstuff, whether these are feedcrop areas, or transport and trade hubs where feed is imported. There is also a shift of species, with production of monogastric species (pigs and poultry, mostly produced in industrial units) growing rapidly, while the growth of ruminant production (cattle, sheep and goats, often raised extensively) slows. Through these shifts, the livestock sector enters into more and direct competition for scarce land, water and other natural resources.

These changes are pushing towards improved efficiency, thus reducing the land area required for livestock production. At the same, time they are marginalising smallholders and pastoralists, increasing inputs and wastes, and increasing and concentrating the pollution created. Widely dispersed non-point sources of pollution are ceding importance to point sources which create more local damage but are more easily regulated.

## Livestock 'devour' and degrade land

The livestock sector is by far the single largest anthropogenic user of land. The total area occupied by grazing is equivalent to 26% of the ice-free terrestrial surface of the planet. In addition, the total area dedicated to feedcrop production (470 million hectares) amounts to 33% of total arable land. In all, livestock production accounts for 70% of all agricultural land and 30% of the land surface of the planet. Such figures are overwhelming and the same accounts for the rise of land use for livestock production as depicted in Figures 1-4.

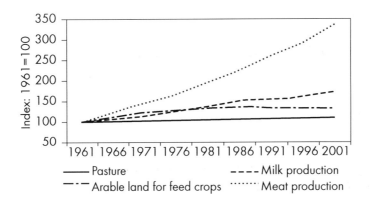

Figure 1. Global trends in land-use area for livestock production and total production of meat and milk.

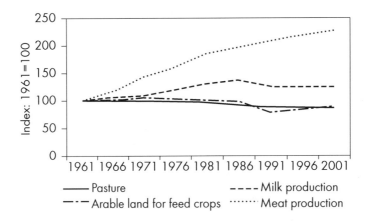

Figure 2. Trends in land-use area for livestock production and total production of meat and milk – EU 15.

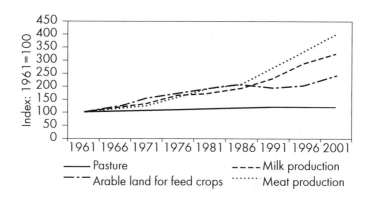

Figure 3. Trends in land-use area for livestock production and total production of meat and milk – South America.

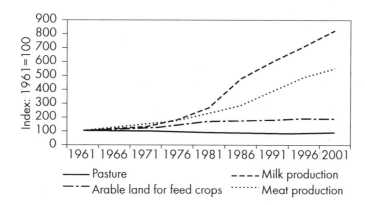

Figure 4. Trends in land-use area for livestock production and total production of meat and milk – East and Southeast Asia.

Expansion of livestock production is a key factor in deforestation, especially in Latin America where the greatest amount of deforestation is occurring – 70% of previous forested land in the Amazon is occupied by pastures, and feedcrops cover a large part of the reminder. About 70% of all grazing land is considered degraded, mostly through overgrazing, compaction and erosion created by livestock action. The dry lands in particular are affected by these trends, as livestock are often the only source of livelihoods for the people living in these areas. Land degradation might reduce the amount of land available for agricultural production in the future.

Overgrazing can be reduced by grazing fees and by removing obstacles to mobility on common property pastures. Land degradation can be limited and reversed through soil conservation methods, better management of grazing systems, limits on uncontrolled burning by pastoralists and controlled exclusion from sensitive areas.

## $CO_2$ and climate

With rising temperatures, rising sea levels, melting icecaps and glaciers and shifting ocean currents and weather patterns, climate change is the most serious challenge facing the human race. The livestock sector is responsible for 18% of greenhouse gas emissions measured in $CO_2$ equivalent. This is a higher share than transport.

The livestock sector accounts for 9% of anthropogenic $CO_2$ emissions. The largest share of this derives from land-use changes – especially deforestation – caused by expansion of pastures and arable land for feedcrops. Livestock are responsible for much larger shares of some gases with far higher potential to warm the atmosphere. The sector emits 37% of anthropogenic methane (with 23 times the global warming potential (GWP) of $CO_2$) most of that from enteric fermentation by ruminants. It emits 65% of anthropogenic nitrous oxide (with 296 times the GWP of $CO_2$), the great majority from manure. Livestock are also responsible for almost two-thirds (64%) of anthropogenic ammonia emissions, which contribute significantly to acid rain and acidification of ecosystems.

*The livestock sector is responsible for 18% of greenhouse gas emissions measured in $CO_2$ equivalent; a higher share than transport*

This high level of emissions opens up large opportunities for climate change mitigation through livestock actions. Intensification – in terms of increased productivity both in livestock production and in feedcrop agriculture – can reduce greenhouse gas emissions from deforestation and pasture degradation. In addition, restoring historical losses of soil carbon through conservation tillage, cover crops, agroforestry and other measures could sequester up to 1.3 tonnes of carbon per hectare per year, with additional amounts available through restoration of desertified pastures. Methane emissions can be reduced through improved diets to reduce enteric fermentation, improved manure management and biogas – which also provide renewable energy. Nitrogen emissions can be reduced through improved diets and manure management.

The Kyoto Protocol's clean development mechanism (CDM) can be used to finance the spread of biogas and silvopastoral initiatives involving afforestation and reforestation. Methodologies should be developed so that the CDM can finance other livestock-related options such as soil carbon sequestration through rehabilitation of degraded pastures.

## Water

The world is moving towards increasing problems of freshwater shortage, scarcity and depletion, with 64% of the world's population expected to live in water-stressed basins by 2025.

The livestock sector is a key player in increasing water use, accounting for over 8% of global human water use, mostly (90%) for the irrigation of feedcrops. It is also probably the largest sectoral source of water pollution, contributing to eutrophication, 'dead' zones in coastal areas, degradation of coral reefs, human health problems, emergence of antibiotic resistance and many others. The major sources of pollution are from animal wastes, antibiotics and hormones, chemicals from tanneries, fertilizers and pesticides used for feedcrops, and sediments from eroded pastures. Global figures are not available but in the United States, with the world's fourth largest land area, livestock are responsible for an estimated 55% of erosion and sediment, 37% of pesticide use, 50% of antibiotic use, and a third of the loads of nitrogen and phosphorus into freshwater resources.

Livestock also affect the replenishment of freshwater by compacting soil, reducing infiltration, degrading the banks of watercourses, drying up floodplains and lowering water tables. Livestock's contribution to deforestation also increases runoff and reduces dry season flows.

Water use can be reduced through improving the efficiency of irrigation systems. Livestock's impact on erosion, sedimentation and water regulation can be addressed by measures against land degradation. Pollution can be tackled through better management of animal waste in industrial production units, better diets to improve nutrient absorption, improved manure management (including biogas) and better use of processed manure on croplands. Industrial livestock production should be decentralised to accessible croplands where wastes can be recycled without overloading soils and freshwater.

Policy measures that would help in reducing water use and pollution include full cost pricing of water (to cover supply costs, as well as economic and environmental externalities), regulatory frameworks for limiting inputs and scale, specifying required equipment and discharge levels, zoning regulations and taxes to discourage large-scale concentrations close to cities, as well as the development of secure water rights and water markets, and participatory management of watersheds.

## Biodiversity

We are in an era of unprecedented threats to biodiversity. The loss of species is estimated to be running 50 to 500 times higher than background rates found in the fossil record. Fifteen out of 24 important ecosystem services are assessed to be in decline.

Livestock now account for about 20% of the total terrestrial animal biomass, and the 30% of the earth's land surface that they now pre-empt was once habitat for wildlife. Indeed, the livestock sector may well be the leading player in the reduction of biodiversity, since it is the major driver of deforestation, as well as one of the leading drivers of land degradation, pollution, climate change, overfishing, sedimentation of coastal areas and facilitation of invasions by alien species. In addition, resource conflicts with pastoralists threaten species of wild predators and also protected areas close to pastures. Meanwhile in developed regions, especially Europe, pastures had become a location of diverse long-established types of ecosystem, many of which are now threatened by pasture abandonment.

Some 306 of the 825 terrestrial ecoregions identified by the Worldwide Fund for Nature (WWF) – ranged across all biomes and all biogeographical realms, reported livestock as one of the current threats. Conservation International has identified 35 global hotspots for biodiversity, characterised by exceptional levels of plant endemism and serious levels of habitat loss. Of these, 23 are reported to be affected by livestock production. An analysis of the authoritative World Conservation Union (IUCN) Red List of Threatened Species shows that most of the world's threatened species are suffering habitat loss where livestock are a factor. According to IUCN the livestock sector is a threat to 1700 endangered species.

Since many of livestock's threats to biodiversity arise from their impact on the main resource sectors (climate, air and water pollution, land degradation and deforestation), major options for mitigation are detailed in those sections. There is also scope for improving pastoralists' interactions with wildlife and parks and raising wildlife species in livestock enterprises.

Reduction of the wildlife area pre-empted by livestock can be achieved by intensification. Protection of wild areas, buffer zones, conservation easements, tax credits and penalties can increase the amount of land where biodiversity conservation is prioritised. Efforts should extend more widely to integrate livestock production and producers into landscape management.

After we have visited briefly the domains of climate, water and biodiversity respectively, Table 1 gives an overview of the environmental impact of the livestock sector.

Table 1. An overview of livestock's environmental impact.

| | Climate | Water | Biodiversity |
|---|---|---|---|
| Pasture and feedcrop expansion into natural ecosystems | +++ | + | +++ |
| Rangeland degradation | +++ | ++ | ++ |
| Contamination in intensive production areas | + | +++ | ++ |
| Intensive feedcrop agriculture | ++ | ++ | ++ |

+++ = large impact; + = small impact

## Cross-cutting policy frameworks

Certain general policy approaches cut across all the above fields. A general conclusion is that improving the resource use efficiency of livestock production can reduce environmental impacts. At the moment, given the substantial inefficiencies in production as well as policy failures, there is still scope for improving efficiency by adopting existing tried and tested technologies. Notwithstanding these opportunities, there is a continuing need for R&D in order to guarantee sustainability in the decades to come.

*A top priority is to achieve prices and fees that reflect the full economic and environmental costs, including all externalities*

While regulations about scale, inputs, wastes and so on can help, a crucial element in achieving greater efficiency is the correct pricing of natural resources such as land, water and use of waste sinks. Many local and global ecosystems are free and underpriced public goods or 'commons'. Livestock producers use these commons to feed their livestock and to dispose their waste. Thereby, they inflict externalities on other current and future users of the commons. As a result, natural resources tend to be overexploited and polluted. This is even aggrevated by perverse subsidies which directly or indirectly encourage livestock producers into environmentally damaging activities.

A top priority is to achieve prices and fees that reflect the full economic and environmental costs, including all externalities. One requirement for prices to influence behaviour is that there should be secure and if possible tradable rights to water, land, use of common land and waste sinks. Damaging subsidies should be removed, and economic and environmental externalities should be built into prices by selective taxing of and/or fees for resource use, inputs and wastes. In some cases direct incentives may be needed.

*It is likely that environmental considerations, along with human health issues, will become the dominant policy considerations for the sector*

Payment for environmental services is an important framework, especially in relation to extensive grazing systems: herders, producers and landowners can be paid for specific environmental services such as regulation of water flows, soil conservation, conservation of natural landscape and wildlife habitats, or sequestration of carbon. Provision of environmental services may emerge as a major purpose of extensive grassland-based production systems.

An important general lesson is that the livestock sector has such deep and wide-ranging environmental impacts that it should rank as one of the leading focuses for environmental policy: efforts here can produce large and multiple payoffs. Indeed, as societies develop, it is likely that environmental considerations, along with human health issues, will become the dominant policy considerations for the sector. Consumers and civil society indeed increasingly command environmental measures. The development of markets for organic products and other forms of eco-labelling are precursors of this trend.

Finally, there is an urgent need to develop suitable institutional and policy frameworks, at local, national and international levels, for the suggested changes to occur. This will require strong political commitment, and increased knowledge and awareness of the environmental risks of continuing 'business as usual' and the environmental benefits of actions in the livestock sector.

# Part 4

# Perspectives on food policy

# Food policy in practice: the case of France

*Egizio Valceschini*

French food policy has three main objectives: to safeguard the safety and health of consumers, to guarantee the reliability of product information, and to reserve a distinctive labelling system for certain products. Even though separate laws and instruments have been developed for these three objectives, there are important similarities between the instruments applied. All instruments are exclusively in the field of economic, social and quality regulation. The national government creates institutional mechanisms and legal frameworks that determine the conditions under which the food supply chain can carry out its activities and that prescribe the physical characteristics food products have to satisfy. These mechanisms take four very different forms: the enactment of minimum quality standards, the enactment of reference standards, the awarding of property rights and the definition of legal responsibilities.

## Food safety law

In France, consumer protection with respect to food safety and hygiene is a key responsibility of the national government. Government intervention is laid down in the law of 1905 protecting against adulteration and fraud. The law still forms the basis of the regulations which are in force today. Government intervention is legitimised by the fact that there is a public requirement to safeguard human life and that health is considered as a public good. The national government is in the best position to effectively preserve and guarantee the safety of its citizens. The government has the necessary legitimacy to defend the citizens. It has the capacity of expertise to draw up standards as well as the power of coercion indispensable for the implementation of effective control mechanisms. Finally, the government's credibility is vital for establishing confidence in the relevance, reliability and efficacy of the regulations.

Food safety is, in principle, simply a matter of minimum quality standards. Even though minimum quality standards enhance market performance and social welfare, the market itself cannot be expected to establish and attain them. Therefore, the logic of the system of standardisation in France is traditionally that the national authorities lay down minimum quality standards that producers are obliged to satisfy in order to gain market access.

In order to enact minimum quality standards, regulatory intervention relies on precise scientific knowledge of the relation between the physical characteristics of food products and human health. Its capacity of expertise must allow it to describe food characteristics, food constituents, manufacturing processes and processing technologies in detail right through to the methods of analysis and control. After codifying this knowledge, it can draft precise instructions (minimum thresholds, for example) and control protocols.

This method is experiencing major difficulties for two reasons. Firstly, it is coming up against the limits of scientific knowledge. Without preliminary codified knowledge, there is no way of drafting rigorous instructions. Faced with poorly understood biochemical processes, such as in the case of pesticide residues in tinned fruits and vegetables, or faced with epidemiological phenomena that are partly unpredictable, such as Bovine Spongiform Encephalopathy (BSE), the enactment of references or thresholds to be respected is not always possible or only with the use of complex application and verification methods. In the end, the regulator's expertise and ability to coerce and control is limited. Secondly, regulatory activity must deal with the exponential growth in the number of products appearing on the market. However, the draft of technical systems of reference, the updating of verification procedures and the actual controls reach such a quantity and degree of complexity (not to mention controversies about innovations, as with GMO's), that the work capacity and skills of the authorities become overburdened.

In the light of these limitations, current French food safety policy is henceforth based on two principles. In the first place, the tasks of risk assessment and risk management are separated. Risk assessment is carried out by the newly established independent French Food Safety Agency (AFSSA). The separation allows political decision makers to take food safety measures (risk management) based on independent expert opinion (risk evaluation). In the second place, and in accordance with EU policy in general, food safety is approached from an integral perspective ('from farm to fork'). This approach implies full coverage of the food supply chain, both at the regulatory and control levels. Moreover, it makes agri-food companies responsible for food safety by requiring the application of HACCP (Hazard Analysis and Critical Control Points).

## Regulation versus standardisation

The requirement to apply HACCP illustrates a major shift in public regulation with respect to food safety. Previously food safety standards not only specified the minimum and maximum levels certain product characteristics had to attain, but also all the measures food companies had to take in order to reach these levels. Now they oblige food companies to apply food safety procedures such as HACCP. Normalisation and standardisation are becoming a complementary tool of regulation (Borraz, 2007). Food companies are free to decide how to assess risks and how to control them. The reason behind this policy change is that food companies are thought to have the technological abilities to assess and control risks in order to regulate themselves. Due to this policy change the burden and responsibility of risk evaluation and management has shifted to private food companies, a task rigidly assumed by the government until now.

However, the new policy approach has generated a new form of uncertainty. In the previous approach, public food safety regulations explicitly laid down all the measures to be taken and the resulting responsibilities and liabilities of food companies. In the new approach, companies' freedom to translate food safety objectives into their own risk assessment and management measures creates uncertainty about the question of whether responsibility and liability requirements are met.

In order to reduce this uncertainty, food companies started complying with such reference standards as ISO 9000. These standards are based on a premise: there is equivalence between the performance of the system and the attainment of food safety objectives (in other words, 'products are safe because systems are effective'). The confidence of the different operators, and in particular that of the customers in their suppliers, is assumed to be guaranteed by this equivalence. But it contains a remarkable paradox: essentially, product specifications distinguish its characteristics while, in contrast, system standards represent generic terms with respect to the production process. A gap between the product specifications and the system standards is, therefore, possible.

*Companies' freedom to translate food safety objectives into their own risk assessment and management measures creates uncertainty*

Food retailers do not tolerate this gap. In order to avoid any risk, they have been developing private reference systems. By developing their own private labels, food retailers commit their name, reputation and liability on the issue of food quality and safety. When a food retailer subcontracts the manufacturing of a product sold under the retailer's brand, he is dependent on the quality of the manufacturer's work. For this reason, it is of strategic importance to monitor the manufacturer's quality. Food retailers are involved in controlling their suppliers by specifying ever more demanding terms of quality, but also by enforcing ever tighter controls. In the first phase, until the early 21st century, every food retailer drew up its own specifications and performed the supplier audits themselves. In a second phase, the food retailers came together to harmonise their specifications and audits. They designed common reference systems which they had checked by certification organisations such as GlobalGAP,

BRC (British Retailers Consortium) and IFS (International Food Standard). These reference systems all define food safety requirements starting from the levels imposed by the regulations (Ménard and Valceschini, 2005).

## Food safety and health concerns

Today's food consumers are not only interested in the protection by standards, thresholds and controls enacted in the name of food safety. It is also a matter of communicating product information that is comprehensible to consumers and helps them to make food choices in accordance with their preferences with respect to, for example, health and taste. The consumers demand the right to judge for themselves what is safe, healthy or tasty. In this respect, consumers are not only interested in food safety information as such, but also in information about nutrition and health claims.

Health concerns are transforming the idea of food safety. Concerns are no longer about the risks of sudden and rapid microbial infection, but about the long-term health effects of potentially harmful food ingredients. With respect to the long-term health effects of food consumption, bacteriological quality criteria are less relevant. The assessment of the long-term health effects of toxic substances or of their accumulation in the body, for example, often leads back to scientific questions that are not yet resolved. Confronted with contradictory information and diverging expert opinions, it is anything but easy for consumers to determine what is harmful, toxic, healthy or beneficial for a good figure. A continuous creation of new products, ingredients and processes adds to this consumer uncertainty.

*Confronted with contradictory information and diverging expert opinions, it is anything but easy for consumers to determine what is harmful, toxic or healthy*

## The policy of quality

For a long time the French authorities have had a voluntary policy of promoting agricultural and food products to be 'original', 'authentic', and of 'superior quality'. Historically, the first legal mechanism to codify a nomination of origin was the *Appellations d'Origine Contrôlées* (AOC) (controlled designations of origin) which was established in 1919. In the sixties this quality policy was primarily a policy of economic compensation for certain categories of farmers in disadvantaged areas. From the end of the eighties onwards, this policy supported an agricultural strategy of differentiation by quality. The origin of the product is considered a token of a quality generating economic value, which has to be protected in much the same way as a commercial brand.

*The origin of the product is considered a token of a quality generating economic value*

The most successful examples of these quality strategies in France were in the wine-producing sector, poultry production and in the cheese sector. Today the law has established four official certifications each of which is based on a particular characteristic of origin. The AOC advances the characteristics of 'typical and authentic taste' of produce that is obtained according to 'traditional' production processes. The *Label Rouge* (red label) underlines 'superior quality' achieved by conforming to production criteria codified in a technical reference system. To give another example, *Agriculture Biologique* (organic agriculture) refers to 'natural' characteristics of a product obtained according to a production system that 'respects the environment'.

The allocation of property rights on terms of origin is based on three mechanisms. Firstly, the definition of quality standards falls within the competence of a body to which the government has delegated public action prerogatives. Quality is managed by a central authority: the *Institut National des Appellations d'Origine* (INAO - National Institute for Designations of Origin), which is the French organisation charged with regulating controlled place names. INAO decides which products are entitled to a denomination and therefore defines the property rights of local producers organisations. INAO also makes sure that the rules are respected by these groups. Secondly, the producers' collective defines the rules concerning the characteristics of production conditions and ensures their members' commitment to them. Thirdly, an independent third party controls the process, and allocates a certification for the origin-based products.

Since the early 1990s this quality policy has been part of a European regulatory framework, in particular the 1992 regulations on AOP (protected designation of origin) and IGP (protected geographical indication). In practice, these regulations are an extension of the principles of the French mechanisms to the EU level. The rationale of the legal and institutional system consists of the specification and protection of exclusive rights of the specific resources used. For this reason, the system codifies the relationship between on the one hand the characteristics of a product, and, on the other hand, the particularities of a region, specific traditional production methods or a local production practices. From the consumers' perspective, characteristics of origin are primarily credence attributes whose credibility depends on the system of guarantees behind the information about the attribute of origin. Certification serves to standardise products and to check that the producers respect their commitments. In this way, it functions like other institutions which define a series of formal or informal rules in order to reduce consumer and supply chain transaction costs (North, 1990).

## The private label challenge

*Certification serves to standardise products and to check that the producers respect their commitments*

Product differentiation is becoming an ever more important strategic variable now food retailers increasingly sell food products under private label. Because retail private labels meet ever higher quality standards, food processors and government supported producer groups face increasing competition. In recent years, food retailers have developed 'quality brands' under private labels which refer to the origin of products or production methods (*Terre et Saveur* from Casino, Auchan's *Filière agriculture raisonnée* or Cora's *Engagement dès l'origine* are just a few French examples).

Until recently, product quality was primarily guaranteed and monitored by the official certifications. Today, the distinction between the government supported quality labels on the one hand and the labels of major food retailers and processors on the other is blurring. Various reasons fuel this tendency. Major food processors and retailers increasingly produce and market food with references to traditional and artisanal features. The quality level of industrially produced mass food is continuously improving. There is convergence of industrial products and traditional products on two characteristics that are at first glance antagonistic: hygiene and taste. Moreover, there is a trend towards industrialising traditional products. Finally, the spread and use of traceability and certification mechanisms may in time raise production standards in the whole agricultural sector.

The efficacy of the quality and origin policy is therefore threatened by brand strategies which resemble the official certifications in three fundamental areas: reference to the origin, traceability of origin, and control by certification. Little by little, the official quality certifications will be absorbed or imitated by the strategies of major industrial manufacturers and distributors. The Carrefour group label or the range of origin-based products 'Reflets de France' perfectly illustrate this development.

## The quest for a balanced diet

In France, as in numerous countries, the prevalence of obesity and overweight is rising dramatically, in particular in the younger generation. In 2006, 29.2% of French adults (16% of children) were overweight, and 12.4% of the adult population (4% of children) were obese. As in many other countries, the overweight phenomenon mainly affects the poorer sectors of society. Overweight and obesity play a role in the development and progression of heart problems and diabetes, and, thus, in the increasing costs of treating these illnesses.

*Major food processors and retailers increasingly produce and market food with references to traditional and artisanal features*

Public health concerns and its financial risks have prompted authorities as well as the agri-food sector and the media to take a much greater interest in food as a factor in the realm of people's health and well-being. As a result, health information targeted on consumers has skyrocketed in recent years. Information is, for example, provided in the form of dietary recommendations, product labels or culinary advice. Industry is responding to this focus on food and health by segmenting the market on the basis of product nutrition characteristics. Functional foods, special diet foods and a variety of health-oriented product indications or labels are nowadays easy to find on the supermarket shelves. However, just offering food consumers information is not enough.

It is a challenge for all private and public stakeholders to provide consumers with information that improves their understanding and learning capacities about the (un)healthiness of what they eat and their food habits.

*The nutritional policy in France is based on 'a balanced diet' which focuses on the major food groups, rather than a nutrient-based approach*

Besides product-centred information, it is considered to be of great importance to focus on the overall diet. The nutritional policy in France is based on 'a balanced diet' which focuses on the major food groups. Rather than a nutrient-based approach, a balanced diet is pivotal in the comprehensive public health programme that was launched in January 2001: the *Programme National Nutrition Santé* (PNNS - Food and Health Plan). The general principle of the PNNS is that the population should be able to benefit from real-life and visible activities allowing them, by improving their diet, to reduce the risk of disease and to optimise their state of health and quality of life, at all stages of life. Several action plans have been defined regarding screening and treating nutritional disorders in the health care system, and measures regarding specific groups. However, the programme is not exclusively concerned with the treatment or screening of pathologies. It is also interested in their prevention through diet by suggesting that nutrition is a major determinant of health.

Even if nutrition is not the sole determinant of the pathologies concerned, it is a factor that the authorities hope to influence on both the collective and individual level by promoting a diet and lifestyle that are favourable to health and to the reduction of the risk of chronic diseases. Within the PNNS, nutrition is about the consumption of food as well as about caloric expenditure via physical activity. Besides its biological function, food consumption has strong cultural, social and emotional aspects. The PNNS therefore involves all the stakeholders in the sector and takes various dimensions of food and eating into account: health, pleasure, culture, economy and trade. Agri-food business, thus, occupies a central place in the PNNS. Once the stakeholders have established a direction, the PNNS promotes messages which rely on scientific expertise arranged by the authorities.

The PNNS strives to meet its objectives by acting simultaneously on the demand (guiding consumers towards a more varied and balanced diet) and supply side (enriching the nutritional composition of foods) of the food market. The instruments used are meant to encourage rather than to compel. They focus on consumer information and education, and on obtaining voluntary commitment from the actors in the supply chain. The preferred tool to help consumers to make healthy food choices more easily was to present them with so-called consumer reference points ('eat at least five fruit or vegetables per day', 'reduce your salt intake'). These reference points intend to make the most recent scientific information accessible and comprehensible to consumers. They do not concentrate on abstract vitamins and fats but on concrete consumption situations and do not lose sight of the fact that food and food choices are also connected with taste, social interaction, or pleasure. On the supply side, PNNS seeks to encourage the development and promotion of foods containing less fat, sugar and salt, and more fibre. It also supports initiatives which try to make fruits and vegetables in all their forms accessible to everyone. Agri-food companies are encouraged to optimise supply both in terms of the nutritional composition of food as well as its presentation and forms of sale, in particular the size of portions. More recently the PNNS has tried to arrange for producers as well as processors, distributors and restaurant owners to commit themselves voluntarily to nutritional progress commitment charters. These commitments comprehend both the change in the nutritional composition of products and the methods of marketing and consumption. They are approved by a committee of independent experts. Participants are allowed to use this government-supported initiative in their marketing. In their turn, PNNS requires the companies to be monitored by third parties as regards the effective implementation of the commitment charters. In addition, an Institute of Food Quality has been established with the aim of monitoring the change in food supply characteristics (using health and economic parameters).

## Limits to public policies

The effects of the initiatives and campaigns developed under the umbrella of PNNS run the risk of being limited. Three possible causes are mentioned here. The first one concerns the absence of positive financial incentives. Campaigns on food supply entrusted to the Ministry of Agriculture and Fisheries aim at promoting the consumption of fruit, vegetables and fish. The Ministry aims at facilitating consumer access to these products – e.g. by providing fruit in schools. A major problem with respect to fruit, vegetables and fish is that they are expensive and do not benefit from aid from the Common Agricultural Policy. A second one stems from the adopted method of standardisation. The above-mentioned commitment charters imply a minimum amount of public control. Simultaneously, it is questionable if these are adequate to meet the health challenges, given the differences in the interests of all the stakeholders involved in the PNNS. The commitment charters refer, among other things, to the obligation of manufacturers to display the ingredients of food products on labels. This obligation could lead to a transfer of consumer purchases from unhealthy to healthy food or could induce food companies to change the content of food products. French authorities are not yet going as far as putting in place negative financial incentive mechanisms, like taxation on very fat, sweet or salty food. Such an option was not chosen, because it could penalise the most disadvantaged consumers, and in addition, challenge the industry's adhesion to the voluntary incentive mechanism of commitment charters. A third limitation has to do with the absence of a European Union policy equivalent to the French policy of a balanced diet. From the French point of view, certain recent international decisions are regarded as significant and positive political signs. This holds true, for instance, for the European Charter on obesity signed by Health Ministers from the European region of the World Health Organisation (2006), WHO's second action plan 2007-2012 in Europe (2007), and the White Paper from the European Commission defining a European strategy to combat health problems related to nutrition, overweight and obesity. Nutritional policies are being followed in several countries, with media campaigns relying on simple messages, sometimes brought to the market by economic stakeholders. EU legislation on nutritional claims or functional foods is in line with the goal to regulate the rapid development of industrial strategies to supply healthy food or food containing a health claim. However, all these activities are centred on nutrients and the information on the products rather than on dietary regimes. The absence of a homogenous European nutrition and health policy is an obstacle to the efficacy of the national balanced diet policy. In comparison to the European food safety policy, which has evolved into a comprehensive and complex instrument, European support for a nutritional policy of a balanced diet is as yet rather incomplete.

# In response to challenges: Canada's agriculture and agri-food policy evolution

*Tulay Yildirim and Margaret Zafiriou*

The policies that govern agriculture and agri-food trade and production in any country are ultimately influenced by the environment in which those policies are developed. Canada's recent experience in developing a new Agricultural Policy Framework (APF) has been no different. The many challenges and opportunities that the sector has been facing arising from the global trading environment, technological change, emerging economies, consumer and market demands and macro-economic factors all have had a role to play in determining the priorities and vision of the APF. Even though the first APF running from 2003 to 2008 came to an end, the APF will continue to influence the policy agenda that is in place over the next five year period (2008-2013). This chapter will attempt to explain how the APF was developed and evolved in response to the various challenges and opportunities facing the sector and how the sector has responded to these challenges.

## Complexity, collaboration and consultation

Policy-making in Canada is a fairly complex process, involving multiple jurisdictions, collaboration with various partners, and extensive consultations with stakeholders. This is because Canada is a Confederation, organised around a strong central federal government and 13 provincial and territorial governments with their own powers. Canada's constitution lays out agriculture as a jurisdiction that is shared between the federal and provincial governments. As a result, agricultural policies can only be developed after broad consensus is reached and there is agreement between the 'feds' and the provinces.

Policy-making also requires the collaboration of the Department of Agriculture and Agri-food with other federal partners, whose mandate is to deal with the regulatory aspects of food production and consumption, such as inspection and safety, the quality of grains, plant and animal health and the health of Canadians. The Department of Agriculture and Agri-food Canada (AAFC), which only expanded to include an agri-food component in its mandate and name in 1994, consequently works with the Canadian Grain Commission, the Canadian Food Inspection Agency, Health Canada and the Public Health Agency of Canada when setting regulatory policies influencing food.

*Supply chain cooperation is increasingly required in the new food economy*

Finally, because of the increasingly complex issues surrounding agriculture and agri-food policy that are often controversial and lead to a polarised debate, policy-making requires extensive consultations with stakeholders and information and expertise to inform the debate and achieve consensus. Stakeholders include producer organisations, commodity associations, industry players and the general public. The Department developed a Value Chain Roundtable (VCRT) process as part of the APF in order for industry to be consulted regularly and to help develop a consensus approach to evolving issues, especially given that supply chain cooperation is increasingly required in the new food economy. The Department also developed mechanisms for strengthening informed dialogue, through the Canadian Agri-food Policy Institute (CAPI) and strengthening policy research capacity, through the Agricultural Policy Research Networks. In this way, stakeholders, policymakers and academics could be brought together to inform the debate and develop consensus on policy issues of concern to the sector.

## Export-orientation and liberalisation

The Canadian agriculture and agri-food system is a dynamic chain of industries that is becoming more and more complex and integrated. It is an important sector given the major contribution it makes to the Canadian economy. In 2007, the total economic output of the

Canadian agriculture and agri-food system, measured as Gross Domestic Product (GDP), rose to 87.9 billion CDN dollars (59.6 billion Euro) in constant 1997 dollars. This represented 8.0% of total Canadian GDP. In terms of employment, there were 2.1 million persons employed in the agriculture and agri-food system, accounting for 12.8% of total Canadian employment or one in eight jobs.

Given that Canada is a small open economy, with a relatively small population (33 million people compared to the US's 330 million population next door), the Canadian agriculture and agri-food sector is very export-oriented and dependent on trade. In 2006, Canada exported approximately 28 billion CDN dollars worth of agriculture and agri-food products, and imported approximately 24 billion CDN dollars. Primary agriculture exports were valued at 10 billion CDN dollars and processed food exports were valued at 18 billion CDN dollars. The major destination of Canadian agriculture and agri-food exports was to the US (58%) followed by Japan (8.5%) and the EU (6.2%). Over the past 15 years, Canadian agriculture and agri-food exports grew significantly, especially in value added terms. Consumer-oriented exports grew from 3 billion CDN dollars in 1990 to 14 billion in 2006 – more than a four-fold increase.

This growth in value-added exports can be attributed to various factors, including trade liberalisation, a favorable exchange rate and substantial industry restructuring and diversification as a result of trade liberalisation. The Uruguay Round of Trade Negotiations finally brought about an Agreement on Agriculture in 1993 that introduced disciplines around export subsidies and production-distorting farm support. Major agricultural trading countries such as the US and the EU, as well as Australia, Japan and Canada agreed to reductions in the levels of agricultural support they provided to their farmers. When this was combined with the Canada-US Free Trade Agreement (CUSTA), negotiated in 1989 and the North American Free Trade Agreement (NAFTA), negotiated between Canada, the US and Mexico in 1992, the result was a significant reduction in trade barriers, an increase in market

*Agriculture and the agri-food system account for 12.8% of total Canadian employment or one in eight jobs*

access and decoupled support to farmers and increased integration of food processing and livestock markets in North America. In Canada, the Farm Income Protection Act in 1991 introduced several support programmes that targeted a Whole Farm approach, meaning income from all farm sources, as opposed to commodity-based price and income stabilisation. This resulted in more decoupled support that was less production-distorting, and that also complied with the new WTO Agreement on Agriculture. One major policy change that accompanied these trade agreements which had a dramatic impact on Canadian agriculture was the elimination of the Western Grain Transportation Act (WGTA) in 1995. Once eliminated, structural change resulting from increased diversification and value-added agriculture on the Prairies took place.

Global developments have created challenges and opportunities for the agriculture and agri-food sector and have also influenced the policies that have been put in place to ensure the sector can remain competitive and profitable. Among the challenges the sector faces that have influenced the development of the APF are emerging low cost competitors, technological change, emerging powerhouse economies, changing consumer and market demands and the increased use of non-tariff barriers to trade.

## Productivity and competitiveness

While Canadian food processors experienced productivity gains in the 1990s relative to other countries, especially the US, they recently have lost their competitive edge. Productivity growth has been slowing relative to competitors, and Canadian food processors increasingly face competition from low cost imports from emerging economies such as China, India, Brazil and Argentina. The emergence of low cost producers has led Canadian producers to experience declining farm income, particularly from the loss of traditional commodity markets. Technological change, including new innovations such as the internet, computerisation, biotechnology, nanotechnology, genomics, just-in-time inventory processes and specialised machinery and equipment (e.g. airseeders), have been contributing to productivity growth and increased agricultural production in Canada and around the world. Technological change has transformed agriculture, leading to increased yields, lower costs of production, new crop and livestock varieties, new farming methods and new innovative food products. But it has also led to increased commodity supplies, particularly in developing countries and a downward trend in real global commodity prices over time.

Canada historically invested significant amounts in the past on public sector R&D in agriculture, but more recently these amounts have been declining, especially as a share of production. In 2006, Canada's public R&D share was estimated at 1.3% of production, a decline from 1.7% in 1990. In food processing, Canada's private sector spends significantly less than other countries on private sector R&D. On the other hand, Canadian food processors benefit from R&D spent elsewhere, such as from the innovation and R&D spending being performed by supply chain partners, such as packaging and ingredients suppliers, including primary inputs. Also, many Canadian food manufacturing companies are benefiting from the R&D that is being conducted by their foreign owners (e.g. Kraft or Nestlé) or through foreign direct investment (FDI) inflows, that rose in Canada after trade liberalisation.

## Product differentiation

Productivity improvements will continue to be important for ensuring that the agriculture and agri-food industry in Canada can remain competitive on world markets. But it is not enough. It is also important for the industry to develop new markets and new products that are innovative and differentiated to meet growing consumer demands from consumers at home and abroad, such as from emerging powerhouse economies, such as China and India.

Changing consumer and market demands have been a major challenge but also an opportunity facing the sector and influencing the recent policy environment. As indicated before in several chapters of this volume, consumers are looking for higher quality in the food items they purchase, including added convenience, taste, nutrition, and other attributes. Food with special processing characteristics that address societal values, such as environmentally-responsible, organic, pesticide free and fair trade products, among other characteristics, are commanding premiums as consumers are willing to pay more for these attributes.

*It is a major challenge for public regulators to act swiftly upon market developments*

The increased demand for foods with specific quality attributes has led to changes in the demand for public regulation as well as to a proliferation of private standards. It is a major challenge for public regulators to act swiftly upon market developments. However, the current regulatory framework in Canada has been blamed for not allowing the quick and flexible approval of new innovative products with quality attributes that consumers are demanding and thereby impeding innovation. As an example, approval for new food products with health benefits, functional foods and nutraceuticals (FFN), are taking as long as seven years to be approved, thereby discouraging innovations. The future agriculture and agri-food policy framework being developed includes regulatory streamlining to try to overcome this impediment.

The proliferation of private standards creates another challenge for policymakers. While government traditionally has created public standards for food safety, increasingly private standards are being developed by large global retailers and food processors to assure quality that, in many cases, are more stringent than public standards, according to a recent survey by the OECD (see also Barbara Fliess's chapter in this book). Most firms have also implemented traceability requirements for food categories prior to any legislation being introduced, such as for horticulture products. All firms surveyed felt capable and better equipped to manage food safety and to respond faster to failures than regulatory authorities. Hence, public and private standards are increasingly working together to assure food safety and quality of food products. Because supply chain coordination serves to reduce transaction costs when food safety and quality assurances are required, supply chain collaboration is becoming increasingly essential at the same time, for efficient markets to work.

## Briefly on new trade barriers and biofuels

The increase in demand for higher quality food products that are safe and come with specific quality assurances are also leading to the increased use of non-tariff barriers to trade (related to sanitary and phytosanitary (SPS) and technical trade issues). These barriers can reduce market access and lead to higher costs for trading countries wishing to comply. As an indicator, the average number of disagreements that were brought to each SPS Committee went up from 5 in 1995 to about 25 in 2001. Perhaps one of the first well-publicised cases where food imports into the EU were impeded by non-tariff measures on food products was the 1986 EU case against American beef which allegedly contained growth hormones. Today, similar such cases are proliferating in world trade. More recent developments have led to even more challenges for the agriculture and agri-food sector. Since 2003, serious animal diseases such as BSE and Avian Influenza found in Canada have led to millions of dollars in lost revenues from border closures, loss of export markets, and animals destroyed.

Recently non-food applications of agricultural commodities attracted major societal and policy concern. This holds notably for the challenges and opportunities of biofuel production imply for agricultural, food and energy markets (see the chapter of Dileep Birur *et al.* in this volume). Most countries have introduced strong government incentives to promote biofuel production, including mandated renewable fuel targets of 5% of transportation fuels for ethanol and 2% for biodiesel in Canada. A major driver behind the move to biofuels has been environmental concerns, given that it is argued that biofuel use produces somewhat lower greenhouse gas emissions. In the United States, energy security is the primary driver, while farm income is important in both the US and Canada.

## The APF and its five pillars

It is in the above-sketched context that new policy frameworks for the agriculture and agri-food sector have been developed in Canada. The year 2003 marked the beginning of a new policy era in Canada. This was when the Agricultural Policy Framework (APF) was implemented for a five year period. After extensive consultations and deliberations, Federal Provincial and Territorial Ministers recently agreed on a new vision for agricultural policy for the 2008-2012 period to address current challenges. New policy measures, which will achieve this new vision, are currently being developed and implemented. Compared to earlier periods, Canadian agriculture and agri-food policy has evolved substantially over the past decade.

The APF was negotiated over a period of two years between the Federal, Provincial and Territorial Ministers of Agriculture. It was developed in response to the challenges discussed above that existed at the time the APF was being conceived, particularly in response to market access issues as world markets were becoming more restrictive, and as many trade issues plagued the marketplace. With reductions in tariff rates being implemented under the WTO, countries used SPS regulations, food safety and quality (FSQ) issues and other factors to restrict access to their domestic markets. The APF attempted to address these challenges with the following vision: to secure the long-term prosperity and success of the agriculture and agri-food sector by being the world leader in food safety, innovation and environmentally-responsible production.

*Compared to earlier periods, Canadian agriculture and agri-food policy has evolved substantially over the past decade*

The APF was aimed, among other things, to target the challenges identified above. By improving quality standards and the private sector's ability to communicate product quality, the Canadian government promoted the supply chain's ability to develop new products and to grasp new market opportunities and addressed possible new trade barriers. By investing in innovation and science, the Canadian government addressed the supply chain's challenges in terms of productivity and competitiveness. Part of the science and innovation programme is targeted at meeting the challenges of the bio-fuel economy. Two of the five pillars established under the APF target food safety and quality and science and innovation. The *Food Safety and Quality* pillar was meant to make Canada the world leader in production, processing and distributing safe and reliable food. The *Science and Innovation* pillar aimed at sustainable development, and innovation that generates profit, and to instill confidence in food safety and quality. Both pillars will be discussed in more detail below.

Three pillars address the environment, the support of small and medium-farm enterprises and risk management respectively. The *Environment* pillar was aimed to achieve environmental sustainability and to monitor the progress made in achieving it. Although it is not treated in depth in this chapter, the environmental programme, of course, had a role in achieving the envisaged environmentally-responsible production. The *Renewal* pillar sought to provide producers with access to information, skills, knowledge and advisory services in order to improve farm business management and help farmers transition out of agriculture. The *Business Risk Management* pillar was meant to help farmers better manage the risks and profitability associated with their farming operations.

All five pillars were linked to the goal to improve Canada's international competitiveness and trade and to remain compliant with international agreements. Steady industry input was secured through a Value Chain Roundtable process, whereby the Department of Agriculture and Agri-food staff consulted with industry players from all levels of the Value Chain based along commodity lines.

## Food safety and quality programme

The Food Safety and Quality (FSQ) programme, first of all, aimed to facilitate the industry to develop and implement government-recognised food safety, quality and traceability systems from 'field to fork'. It built on already existing on-farm and post-farm programmes, building on an integrated approach to food safety along the supply chain. Programme elements under the FSQ pillar focused on three elements: (1) system development for food safety, food quality and traceability throughout the entire food chain; (2) on farm implementation of these systems; and (3) outreach and training for industry players to facilitate uptake of these FSQ initiatives.

System development was meant to promote food safety, food quality and traceability. Food safety has been enhanced by reducing exposure to hazards using the definitions and principles of the Hazard Analysis and Critical Control Points (HACCP). Food safety policy was extended to On-Farm Food Safety, to ensure the elimination of hazards as far back as the farm level, in addition to the food processing, retailing and food service levels. Policy with respect to food quality focused on meeting or exceeding market requirements.

*Policy with respect to food quality focused on meeting or exceeding market requirements*

Food quality is defined by the International Standards Organisation (ISO) as 'the totality of features and characteristics of a product'. This can include product 'content' attributes such as nutrition or 'process' attributes such as pesticide-free, organic or genetically modified. In some of these cases, private standards have been developed to ensure conformity and in others, public standards have been developed. The extent of government involvement in food quality will vary depending on the extent to which public standards will be required. The traceability element encouraged the development of processes that can trace the history, location, age and associated food safety and quality standards of food products from field to fork.

Building on the FSQ systems developed, the on-farm implementation programme focused on helping famers to implement food safety systems based on HACCP principles. The Food Safety Initiative, focused on helping the provinces and industry move toward a national standard of HACCP and good manufacturing practices in non-federally registered processing plants, as well as research, outreach and staff training to strengthen provincial food safety infrastructure by supporting provincial governments.

## Targets achieved

Now that the five year time period for the APF is over, there have been efforts to look back and evaluate how successful the APF has been at achieving its targets. About 20 national commodity organisations that participate on the Canadian On-Farm Food Safety Working Group have cooperated to develop common tools for their respective on-farm safety programmes. Cattle, hogs, poultry and horticulture producer associations all have introduced programmes for on-farm food safety. In addition, under this pillar, AAFC's Research Branch initiated a virology programme, which has resulted in the publication of a Compendium of Official Methods for the detection of food borne viruses, strengthened resources in food microbiology and molecular genetics, and linked scientists nationally to work together in support of the national food safety and quality initiatives.

Two outcomes under the FSQ pillar which are particularly worth mentioning include the Canadian Cattle Identification Programme (CCIP) and the introduction of Mandatory National Organic Standards. The CCIP is an industry-led initiative that established a trace-back system designed for the containment and eradication of animal disease. The Canadian Cattle Identification Agency, which helped implement this programme, showed great foresight in putting in place the initial key elements of a traceability system (mandatory identification of cattle and bison) as early as 1998. This comprehensive, integrated national animal tracking system, offers Canadian producers a significant competitive advantage through the development of the Can-Trace Canadian Food Traceability Data Standard and the publication of the Can-Trace Roadmap. This plan identifies the industry action plans for adopting a harmonised approach to food product traceability from field-to-fork. In many ways, this was instrumental in ensuring that after the BSE cow was found in Canada in May 2003, that damage to Canadian export markets and Canada's reputation as a country with world-class disease surveillance and science-based systems to ensure the health and safety of consumers, were not completely destroyed.

The second outcome that is noticable is the introduction of mandatory National Organic standards that will cover standards, third party accreditation and certification, a national logo, and enforcement of organic products. The development of mandatory standards came at the request and efforts of industry. There will be a two year transition period, after which organic producers must comply with the mandatory standards in order to label products 'organic' in Canada. The motivation behind the move to mandatory standards, after having agreed to voluntary standards in 1998, is to prepare Canadian organic producers to be able to export to the EU, where legislation was recently revised to ensure 'third country' equivalency before imports would be allowed in. Previously, self-regulated voluntary national standards were in place in Canada in all provinces but Quebec, which set the minimum criteria for agricultural practices, food products, management practices and labelling claims. In 2006, organic sales at retail were estimated at 1 billion CDN dollars in Canada, and the market was growing by 20% a year. However, the bulk of organic products are imported. So the mandatory standards will help achieve consumer protection against misleading labelling practices, continued market access to the EU, development of the domestic market and a level playing field for domestic and imported products.

*Bring people and organisations together with a mutual interest in developing new business strategies and market opportunities*

## The science and innovation programme and its results

The Science and Innovation programme aimed to improve the competitiveness of the industry through technological advancement and innovation. There were two major components under this pillar. The first component involved a realignment of public sector R&D resources in science, including the development of an Intellectual Property Rights strategy and a bio-based economy investment strategy. The second component involved programmes to strengthen market chain linkages and encourage the adoption of new innovations (commercialisation) including. The *Broker Programme* aimed to bring people and organisations together with a mutual interest in developing new business strategies and market opportunities. Groups formed through this programme were to build links and identify opportunities to accelerate innovation in areas of commercial and scientific promise for Canada. This resulted in new market opportunities for higher value, agri-based products and processes. The *Agri-Innovation Programme* aimed to provide start-up help for centres of innovation and financial support to advance initiatives, including ones identified through the Broker Programme. It provided funding assistance towards identifying key agri-innovation opportunities; undertaking applied scientific and pilot processing activities, and accelerating the development of new and emerging innovations that offer promise in the market place.

As a result of spending under the Science and Innovation pillar, several results have been achieved. First of all, the programme helped accelerate the development of a wide range of new industrial, health and nutritional products obtained from plants, animals and micro-organisms, through AAFC initiatives such as Flax 2015, Soy 20/20 and Vinifera for life. Other initiatives related to Bioproducts and Bioprocesses were launched and a Science and Innovation Strategy was developed that was based on sector-wide consultations.

In addition to these initiatives, further investments have been made on top of APF funding to promote R&D and commercialisation of bioproducts and biofuels. For example, the Agricultural Bioproducts Innovation Programme (ABIP) aims to promote research, development, technological transfer and commercialisation activity in agricultural bioproducts in Canada through research networks comprising a critical mass of intellectual capacity. The Biofuels Opportunity for Producers Initiative (BOPI) is designed to provide farmers and rural communities with opportunities to participate in and benefit from increased Canadian biofuel production. In addition to these programmes, the Canadian federal government introduced consumption and production incentives for renewable fuel aimed at achieving a 5% ethanol target in transportation fuel by 2010 and a 2% biodiesel target. Most provinces have also introduced provincial programmes along the same line.

## A concise evaluation of APF 1.0

With the 2003-2007 APF just behind, it has been important to take stock of the successes and the failures of the policies and programmes that were a part of this framework. Several reviews have been undertaken and programme performance evaluated. It has been shown that the APF did indeed help the sector change focus to respond to the challenges arising from the global market place, technological change, emerging competitors and changing consumer and market demands, by making use of science to innovate and by introducing food safety and quality systems, promoting environmentally-responsible production practices, while managing the economic performance of the sector. However, at the same time, implementation of the non-risk management elements of the APF has been slower than anticipated and the effort assigned to various elements has been uneven. Moreover, it was also concluded that there is a need to better link the various policy elements of the APF.

*A competitive and innovative sector understands consumer demands, adapts and innovates, promotes innovation and marketing strategies, and collaborates across the chain*

In conclusion, therefore, the main lessons learned from the APF include: better links are required to balance across various policy pillars, implementation of the non-risk management elements of the APF has been slow because of the lack of supporting regulatory and institutional structures that are conducive to deliver on all policy pillars, and involvement and cooperation across all levels of government and industry have been and continue to be crucial in the development of the next generation agricultural policy framework. A competitive and innovative sector will be one that understands consumer demands, adapts and innovates, promotes innovation and marketing strategies, and collaborates across the chain. Clearly, more investment is needed in science and innovation and R&D to improve the competitiveness of the sector.

## The next generation APF: growing forward

When Federal-Provincial-Territorial Ministers of Agriculture met in June 2007, they agreed to the following vision for the Next Generation Agricultural Policy Framework: 'A profitable and innovative agriculture, agri-food and agri-based products industry that seizes opportunities in responding to market demands and contributes to the health and well-being of Canadians'. This vision was developed after having consulted broadly across the country and with a large selection of stakeholders. It was developed to address many of the same challenges that were addressed five years ago with the APF. However, new challenges such as the emergence of developing economies, the escalation of product standards, and new societal concerns over production practices are all forcing governments to consider new policies to address these challenges. Canada, as an exporting country, is also facing an added challenge, and that is the fact that the Canadian dollar has continued to appreciate so that it has now reached and risen above par with the US This is having adverse effects on commodity markets and many manufacturing industries in Canada including food, beverage and tobacco processing, where exports have declined substantially.

One of the important lessons that were learned from the 2003-2007 APF, was the need to better link and balance the policy goals of the framework, and this will be done in the future by targeting (1) competitiveness and innovativeness, and (2) responsiveness with respect to consumer and societal demands. The next programme also seeks to promote pro-activity with respect to risk management.

## Competitiveness, innovativeness and responsiveness

In order to promote the competitiveness and innovativeness of Canadian agriculture and agri-food, the new policy framework must focus on various measures that improve market access to markets, in particular grow markets. Policy programmes should promote export readiness and market development, foster innovation from mind to market through research and commercialisation ideas from around the globe and support business planning and entrepreneurship. Various approaches under the Growing Forward Framework will be needed to address these objectives. Export readiness and market development may be promoted by gathering and disseminating market intelligence in order to evaluate and respond to emerging consumer demand and by developing foresight capacity in the sector to anticipate future opportunities and challenges. Business planning and entrepreneurship may be enhanced by encouraging value chain partnerships. Innovation may be fostered by facilitating the advancement of emerging technology and by promoting private-public R&D partnerships addressing shared priorities. At the same time, public administrations should implement measures modernising regulatory systems and improving regulatory cooperation.

*The sector's responsiveness should address consumer and societal demands with respect to health and wellness on the one hand and the environment and animal care on the other hand*

In order to enhance the responsiveness of the Canadian food supply chain with respect to consumer and societal demands, policies under the Growing Forward Framework must enable the sector to meet and exceed standards and requirements notably those relating to food safety and the environment while building profitability in the industry. This will be achieved by modernising and implementing innovative regulations and standards in a manner that ensures society's needs are met and that contributes to the sector's competitiveness, while providing incentives to encourage the sector to take food safety and environmental action beyond what is enforced by legislation. The sector's responsiveness should address consumer and societal demands with respect to health and wellness on the one hand and the environment and animal care on the other hand. Note that when developing new regulations and standards the impact on costs and competitiveness should be recognised.

## Lessons learned

Both external and internal factors have played a significant role on the evolution of agricultural and agri-food policy in Canada as well as on the structural adjustments in the sector. The result has been a sector that has undergone significant restructuring, become increasingly export-oriented, productive, and consolidated but also increasingly integrated along the supply chain. The sector will continue to face new challenges requiring a continuous need for revisiting and revising policies.

Two major lessons may be drawn from past policy development. First, policy changes that will help the sector address current challenges and prepare the sector for the future require substantial consultations and dialogue in order to achieve understanding of the issues and agreement on solutions. This is because policy changes, invariably lead to redistribution of wealth (winners and losers). Second, it is crucial to have the regulatory and institutional structures in place that are conducive to implementing new policies in order to achieve the desired policy outcomes.

Given the lessons that have been learned in the past, the new Policy Framework, Growing Forward, puts a lot of emphasis on these two issues, and hopefully, we will learn from our previous policy mistakes to develop future policies that will prepare the sector for the opportunities that are there for the taking.

# Food for thought: setting the food policy's research agenda

*Loek Boonekamp, Bruce Lee and Hans Dagevos*

A common theme in this book is that contemporary transformations of agro-food systems and the institutional environments in which these operate as well as profound changes in food lifestyles require a broadening of the scope of both academic attention and policymaking. Within this overall theme, we turn in this chapter to some of the implications for research and issues with respect to informing any ensuing policy debate. We take the Organisation for Economic Cooperation and Development (OECD) and Australian research programmes as examples to get a glimpse of the future. We hope the remainder provides some inspiring ideas about important research topics that meet the challenges of today and tomorrow.

## A changing food system and its research priorities: balance of power

A substantial change has occurred in the agro-food sector over recent decades as firms and farms have grown larger and markets have become more concentrated. Similar to developments in other sectors, firms in the food industry are undertaking strategic alliances, mergers and acquisitions both in the same product family and across sectors. For example, food retailing in Europe, Australia and Latin America is highly concentrated with the top 5 firms accounting for upwards of 60 to 90% of sales. In food processing the configuration is similar and even if the trend is somewhat slower in farming, this sector, too, is becoming more concentrated. However, the farm sector remains characterised by much larger numbers of farms than the number of firms in processing or retailing. This tendency warrants priority being given to research into the balance of power in the food supply chain. OECD research that examines the balance of power in the food chain has focused on the possible impacts of retailer concentration on stakeholders in the meat sector (OECD, 2006). It found that while concentration has grown, there is no conclusive evidence of a recent deterioration in farm returns and that there is no systematic fall in the average farm to retail price spread. The price analysis in four case-study countries (Canada, the Czech Republic, Japan and the Netherlands) shows that food retailers on the whole make little profit on meat although it is sometimes larger for beef. It also appeared that price developments at farm, wholesale and retail level are related to each other, although the extent to which this is the case and the speed of price transmission differs between countries and types of meat. Despite the fact that retailers sometimes make substantial profits on beef, in particular in Canada and Japan, the results of this study do not provide strong evidence of the abuse of market power in the meat sector in these four countries.

The OECD also looked into market power issues in agriculture in a broader sense (OECD, 2005). One issue covered in the study was market power in the food chain. The report came to some relevant conclusions. Firstly, it was stated that no special antitrust laws or enforcement rules relating to monopoly buying are necessary. This is because existing tools used to address monopoly buying are sufficient. Secondly, the study found that the existence of asymmetric price responses to cost increases and cost decreases does not necessarily imply market power by purchasers. Nevertheless, the study recommended, thirdly, that retailer and processor mergers must be carefully analysed to verify whether the first two conclusions remain valid.

## A changing food system and its research priorities: high-tech

Another massive change in the supply side of the food system is the use of science and advanced technologies in generating new processes and products. Biotechnologies that provide new consumer-oriented food traits and more rapid development of varieties may further boost the array of products available. Furthermore, the expanding use of information and communication technologies throughout the food supply chain is modifying company behaviour. Supply logistics which can provide frameworks for tracing and tracking, while getting food to consumers more quickly, more cheaply and more safely are changing the size of the market by shrinking the time distance between production and consumption. Within this context it is entirely understandable that one of the national research priorities set out by the Australian Federal Government focuses on frontier technologies. In 2003 the Australian Government launched the National Research Flagship programme, one of Australia's largest scientific research programmes, in which food is one of the areas of focus. The Food Futures National Research Flagship includes a research portfolio on frontier technologies in the areas of grains, beef, aquaculture, feeds and food processing for new foods and ingredients.

*The expanding use of information and communication technologies throughout the food supply chain is modifying company behaviour*

In order to give an impression of the broad scope and high-tech innovativeness of The Food Futures Flagship, we will briefly elaborate on its components.

The goal of the Future Grains theme, for example, is to redesign the composition of grains to deliver premium grain, grain-based food and feed products with enhanced product quality attributes and benefits for human health. New varieties of wheat are being developed that have high levels of amylose, a form of resistant starch, and a low glycaemic index (Regina *et al.*, 2006). This work has involved the use of RNAi gene silencing techniques to suppress the expression of starch-branching enzymes. The wheat produced has been field tested and has a significantly altered starch composition, increasing the amount of amylose from around 25% up to 70%. Amylose is a form of starch that is more resistant to digestion in the small intestine, providing the potential for the new wheat to be an important component in foods with a low glycaemic index, and favourable attributes that promote bowel health and potentially reduce the risk of colorectal cancer. Due to their high amylose content, these grains also have the potential to be used in environmentally friendly packaging. Other work on this theme is directed at developing grains with altered levels of non-starch polysaccharides such as arabinoxylans and $(1,3;1,4)$-β-glucans and substantiating the health benefits of foods made with these grains. Coeliac-friendly cereals are also being researched to address this lifelong immune disease caused by a reaction to dietary gluten. In oilseed crops research is aimed at developing varieties of canola and cotton with high levels of long-chain omega-3 fatty acids. The long chain omega-3 LC-PUFA, Eicosapentaenoic acid (EPA) and Docosahexaenoic acid (DHA) have been shown to have a range of specific health benefits, for example, positive benefits for cardiovascular disease, optimal brain function and eye development.

The goal of the breed engineering theme is to boost the value of Australia's animal-based food industries for beef and seafood with the application of breed engineering and leading edge production technologies. In beef research, new and modified breeding systems are being developed to increase growth rate, yield and quality of the northern Australian beef herd. The Flagship is exploring the use of testis stem cell transfer technology as a means of converting the majority of the north Australian beef herd into hybrids, combining both high meat quality and performance in tropical conditions. In aquaculture, the Flagship's efforts are focused on prawns, salmon, and abalone. Both quantitative genetics and the use of advanced reproductive technologies, such as gender and ploidy manipulation, are being used. In each of these species, genes and gene markers are being identified that account for population variation in key traits that underpin the eating quality of the food products.

The theme of Designed Food and Biomaterials focuses on three major areas: natural plant structured foods and bioactives, concentrated protein structure and design and energy controlled foods. In the first area the research involves developing an understanding of plant cell tissue microstructure and its modification by conventional and emerging processing technologies, which will enable the preservation of the inherent nutrients and health benefits of fruit and vegetables. High Pressure Processing represents an alternative to chemical and thermal modification of components and ingredients and has been used to develop high quality refrigerated or 'chilled' foods with an extended shelf life. Melons and carrots have been used as model species to investigate the impact of minimal processing on fruit and vegetable eating quality and nutritional status as well as determining the safety, stability and freshness of the foods. The research focuses on composition and architecture of plant cell components and how they are related to nutrient bioavailability, textural and sensory properties: process-dependent changes in fruit and vegetable structure and material behaviour including cell wall and food matrix structures to deliver nutrients into the body and enhance bioavailability. In the second area of concentrated proteins, the research is aimed at building a set of design rules to allow ingredient and food industries to choose specific proteins for functionality. The Commonwealth Scientific and Industrial Research Organisation (CSIRO) has assembled a world leading team of international and Australian scientists to conduct fundamental research on food proteins, backed by cutting edge analytical capability. In the third area of the energy controlled foods project the goal is to develop effective technologies for achieving fat reduction for both commodity and manufactured foods, such as meat, cheese, bakery, snacks and other fat-based foods. The project extends across the whole R&D spectrum, from developing a fundamental understanding as to the role of fat in texture and flavour perception, through to the development and utilisation of innovative fat replacement technologies and their incorporation into real food systems. In this way it will be possible to design and deliver food products to the industry with a significant reduction in energy load without compromising on quality.

*The human nose combines versatility and performance which is unmatched by any scientific instrument*

The fourth and final theme of the Food Futures Flagship programme is called Quality Biosensors and aims to develop a biosensor to measure and optimise flavour throughout the wine-making process (from vineyard to bottle) to meet consumer preferences. Currently, in winemaking, the instruments used to measure aroma are the noses of grape-growers, winemakers or sensory panels. The human nose combines versatility and performance which is unmatched by any scientific instrument. However, it is neither very reproducible nor quantitative. Instruments used to supplement the human nose generally do not approach the overall performance of a well-trained human nose. No combination of sensors available today has the selective sensitivity or discriminating power of the human nose. To address this failing, the Flagship is developing a portable instrument, The Cybernose®, that combines the advantages of a trained human nose with the robustness and quantitative capability of current state-of-the-art analytical instrumentation.

## A changing food system and its research priorities: private standards

Another new area of research that may be addressed concerns the role for public-private cooperation and initiatives in the agro-food sector. The identification of issues by the private sector and the actions it takes subsequently raises the basic questions as to who is best in governing the agro-food system and what roles can be envisaged and would be best suited for government in these public-private partnerships. Public-private interaction also raises questions regarding what the implications are for the more traditional government policy outside such partnerships.

*The identification of issues by the private sector and the actions it takes subsequently raises the basic questions as to who is best in governing the agro-food system*

With respect to this field of research, the OECD carried out a study on private voluntary standards and their growing role in shaping the agro-food system (OECD, 2006b). This work was based on interviews and surveys with those who set the standards and require compliance with them as well as those who must comply, that is to say primary producers. The results indicated that certain private standards schemes are used to achieve product differentiation. But more recently they have become a way to insure compliance with food safety standards and to reassure consumers on specific product and production process attributes. Retailers have to a large extent harmonised their product and process requirements through specific standard schemes. This should in principal reduce transactions costs for buyers and sellers and facilitate worldwide sourcing. But these private standards are stringent and often more demanding than government requirements. Even though they are voluntary in nature, they become de facto compulsory because those suppliers who cannot meet the standard will be excluded from access to the value chain.

The second area of work on private voluntary standards focused on the implications of these standards for developing country access to markets in developed economies (OECD, 2007). Again, this analysis was based on interviews, *Public standards remain* but this time with exporters, producers and importers. *necessary where market* Exclusion from the value chain because of the inability *failures need to be* of producers to comply with industry standards is a *corrected* relatively more important issue for small producers and particularly so for those in developing countries. This study found that where developing country producers have been successful in accessing the international value chain, exporters were playing a key role in transmitting supply requirements to producers and in ensuring that these were complied with. In addition, governments in the more successful developing countries were playing an important role through the provision of an appropriate infrastructure that enables producers and exporters to operate competitively and efficiently in world markets.

Despite the fact that private standards are often more demanding than public standards and have other advantages such as being more flexible and responsive to changing conditions, public standards remain necessary where market failures need to be corrected. Private standards are developed to complement public ones, to reduce transactions costs and improve efficiency in the food chain or to differentiate products. Nevertheless, the question remains as to whether, in certain circumstances, the growing use of private standards may not reflect the lack of government action or may even be a discrete move to let the private sector take on more responsibility. In that case, the government's role would become more one of providing oversight, ensuring that behaviours of different agents in the food chain meet the needs of consumers and society.

## A changing food system and its research priorities: consumer society

The words 'needs of consumers and society' brings us immediately to the next domain of study that is of great importance. Last but not least, we would like to point to changes on the demand side as a research area that deserves full attention.

It is clear that the food system operates in a globalising consumer society in which incomes have been rising while urbanisation and changes in demographics and labour force participation have contributed to modifying food consumption habits. Access to food is no longer an issue in the affluent societies where the emphasis has shifted to safety, quality and variety as well as healthfulness of food products. For this reason it is vital to understand major consumer trends of convenience, taste, nutrition and health in their global context.

From the perspective of the growing prevalence of overweight and obesity worldwide, the issue of food and health has high priority. The current obesity epidemic is a good example of a new blip on many researchers' and policymakers' radar screens that was not there a decade ago. Today, the relationship between diet and health is coming to the forefront of both scholarly and policy debates. In research, questions that currently acquire importance concern the relationship between food and health within the context of today's full-blown consumer society: are we living in an obesogenic society and what are the consequences thereof? Research is also devoted to the complexity of the issue of (un)healthy diets. That is, individual health is determined by a myriad of factors which stretch across economic sectors and requires analytical input from a variety of disciplines. A particularly relevant issue in policy debate regards what the strength and effectivity of government initiatives are in the area of diet, health and nutrition.

The topic of overweight and obesity clearly illustrates that the basic framework of agricultural policymakers needs to be extended. At least it seems clear that it is no longer sufficient to be concerned solely about the farm sector or farmers. Spill-overs into other domains that in many cases extend much further downstream or upstream than the farm gate need to be considered.

Another trend in recent years is the growing emphasis given by consumers and society to production attributes such as sustainability, environmental effects, animal welfare, labour conditions and fair trade (other chapters of this book elaborate on these topics). Research, therefore, needs to focus on understanding and addressing the awareness of consumers regarding the environmental impacts of food production and processing. It should be recognised that consumers and society hold firms, farmers and governments accountable if food is produced that does not satisfy their expectations in terms of these attributes. The voice of consumers and society is beginning to be heard in the governance of the food system, from consultations on policy formulation and new technologies to new forms of consumer assurance. Demand is growing for *The voice of consumers* food with a greater service component as consumers *and society is beginning* evaluate the trade-offs between costs in time and energy *to be heard in the* devoted to meal preparation on the one hand and other *governance of the food* activities on the other hand. Finally, consumers search *system* for foods that meet several criteria simultaneously and this continues to provide further opportunities for product and process innovation in the food supply sector. In order to anticipate consumer demand efficiently and respond to market opportunities competitively, the food industry has no choice but to constantly re-structure, reorganise, and 're-socialise' itself.

# Part 5

# Conclusion

# Anticipating the future of the food economy

*Frank Bunte and Hans Dagevos*

> *There was nothing wrong with being the one who always pointed out that things were more complex than supposed: it was a perfectly honourable and even necessary job. –* (Heller, 2008: 32)

The overall lesson of the foregoing chapters in this book is that the food economy is broad and complex. As emphasised throughout this concise edited collection, the expanding food economy is not only reflected in its global span but also in its incorporation of issues that were previously considered as external to the ins and outs of food economics. Especially the impact and importance of more elusive elements such as trust, integrity, corporate social responsibility, emotions and ethical values in the ways we eat, or transparency are worth mentioning in this respect. Simultaneously with the growing size of the envelope that contains the food economy, to paraphrase Jean Kinsey's words, it becomes more interdependent. The current economic downturn clearly shows that agricultural and food markets have become ever more interwoven. Formerly geographically separated markets have been integrated in such a way that they are nowadays highly sensitive to relatively small changes in demand and supply conditions. In this respect, the food system resembles what is known in the sciences of complexity as the butterfly effect: a system's high sensitivity to fluctuations is metaphorically specified by the flap of a butterfly's wing that sets off a tornado. Without discussing whether the food economy is complex in the scientific sense of the word, it is indeed complex in terms of common parlance. As already discussed at length in the introductory chapter, today's food economy covers issues and phenomena that appear to be separate, but are in fact interconnected and mutually influence one another. Bidirectional tendencies and binary notions are salient characteristics of the modern food economy. Polarities such as globalisation and regionalisation, hardware and software, public and private, fast food and slow food, high tech and authentic, or hedonism and health are part and parcel of the food economy of today and tomorrow. In line with this theme, we start our forward-looking analysis in this concluding chapter with a few bipolarities (abundance and scarcity, giants and dwarfs, civil concerns and everyday practices). After this, we briefly take information and communication technologies (ICT) into account – an issue that has been paid only limited attention to in this volume.

*Because the world economy is increasingly interdependent, scarcity in one market has direct and immediate consequences for scarcity in other markets*

The final pages are devoted to issues and challenges which have been discussed more extensively in the chapters of this edited book. We hope that the issues raised and the challenges shown are instructive and helpful for understanding the current food economy as well as for picturing its not too distant future.

## The dance of abundance and scarcity

Globalisation is likely to continue, with time and distance shrinking due to the fall in travel and transportation costs, with the advancement of information technology as well as with the liberalisation of trade and investment. Agricultural and food markets may be expected to be opened up further if current proposals at the Doha round are implemented and if the proliferation of bilateral and regional trade and investment agreements continues (see the chapter by Frank Bunte). Because the world economy is increasingly interdependent, scarcity in one market has direct and immediate consequences for scarcity in other markets.

Food abundance in OECD countries coincides with food scarcity in developing countries. Or to put it another way, the epidemic proportions that obesity is reaching globally coincides with hunger and malnutrition in many parts of the (developing) world. At the same time, many medium income developing countries such as China, India and Brazil are increasingly able to satisfy the demands of their middle and lower classes for a better material life including protein rich diets. Because protein rich diets require vast amounts of feed and land, agricultural commodities are likely to remain relatively scarce in the decades to come. As a result, food security and access to raw materials are again strategic issues on the policy agenda.

Even though food remains relatively scarce, agricultural commodities are increasingly used as an energy source, especially in developed countries. Governments in developed countries actively promote bio-fuel production in order to fight energy scarcity and energy imports and to meet environmental targets. The growth of bio-fuel production in the US and Europe has led to the decline of US net exports of corn and a growth of EU imports of oilseeds (see the chapter by Dileep Birur *et al.*). The supply of corn and oilseeds to other geographical markets has fallen and world prices of corn and oilseeds have risen accordingly. By addressing scarcity in Western energy markets, scarcity is exacerbated in the world's food markets. The rise in world food prices due to the growth of food and feed consumption in Asia and bio-fuel consumption in the US and Europe does not make the challenge for the least developed countries to fight hunger and malnutrition any easier.

## Giants and dwarfs

At the industry level, the globalisation process may be expected to simultaneously foster industry concentration and the proliferation of small and medium-sized enterprises. The opening up of markets enables multinationals to reap economies of scale and scope and to enlarge cost and price differences with small and medium-sized national enterprises. A limited number of generalist food processors and retailers may be expected to dominate the core of the world's food markets. Multinationals increasingly source globally and slice up supply chain activities in such a way as to minimise supply chain costs. On the other hand, growing demand for variety creates ample opportunity for small and medium-sized enterprises to meet consumer demand for product differentiation. This allows the proliferation of such niche products as organic and regional products (see the chapter by Arjen van Witteloostuijn).

The performance of food companies depends on the match between their strategies (postures) and supply and demand conditions. Multinationals will dominate markets with substantial economies of scale and scope and a large, relatively homogeneous demand, as is the case in, for instance, the markets for sugar, salt, food ingredients and pilsners (economies of scale) or the market for ice cream (economies of scope). Small and medium-sized companies thrive in markets where economies of scale are negligible and consumer demand is heterogeneous, as is the case in, for instance, the markets for bread, confectionery and specialty beers. Because economies of scale tend to diminish over time and the demand for variety increases, one may expect small and medium-sized food companies to play important roles in the food economy of the foreseeable future.

## Civil concerns and everyday practices

*If mankind is not able to manage production in general, and agricultural production in particular, more sustainably, environmental and agricultural resources are most likely to become even more scarce in the future*

Agricultural commodities are likely to remain scarce in the decades to come, because the supply of agricultural commodities faces two major bottlenecks. First, there are not many opportunities in the world outside South America to increase the amount of land used in agricultural production. Second, agricultural production is endangered by environmental stress including greenhouse gas emissions, land degradation, the loss of biodiversity and the availability of clean water (see the chapter by Henning Steinfeld). Current agricultural production is actually among the main contributors to environmental degradation. Encouraged by ill-defined property rights and externalities, scarce natural resources are overexploited. If mankind is not able to manage production in general and agricultural production in particular more sustainably, environmental and agricultural resources are most likely to become even more scarce in the future.

Small wonder that both within the agrofood-complex and society at large the attention to environmental problems and the ecological damage done by the food economy is growing. As a result, sustainability is on the agenda of all major stakeholders, corporations, governments, NGOs, citizens and consumers. They increasingly put forward demands with respect to environmental and societal aspects of food production and distribution as well as with respect to agricultural, food and energy policies. But while public concerns about both the supply and demand side of the food economy gain momentum, a gap remains between such civil concerns and actual behaviour in everyday production and consumption practices. Although corporate social responsibility (CSR) has undoubtedly made its way into the boardrooms of many agrofood companies, more often than not it is neither always easy nor automatically intentional to put one's money where one's mouth is. Consumers, on their part, may have various reasons for neither always nor automatically translating consumer concerns into purchasing behaviour. Taste, convenience, availability or price may be more decisive than social responsibility.

Moreover, lack of information can also be a reason for not consuming 'green' or 'ethical'. With respect to informing consumers about aspects of the production practices of particular (un)branded food items, certification and label programmes play a key role. Labels convey the information that a certain product standard is met. Because labels are a simple device for providing information, they are powerful. However, labels do not give consumers all the information. The criteria underlying the standards are typically unknown. Another shortcoming is that an overabundance of labels on food products easily confuses consumers. More generally, CSR reporting is not well-developed for commodity-type categories such as fresh fish and cut flowers (see the chapter by Barbara Fliess). In everyday practice, CSR is not suitable for building company reputations in such food categories. Neither is information on CSR standards readily available for consumers at the moment. The provision of factual information about key process characteristics is one of tomorrow's challenges for competitive product differentiation in food.

## The information age

We have already mentioned in the introductory chapter that this book's aim is not to be exhaustive but that the previous chapters of this volume take a selection of topics and trends into account. One of the subjects that has received limited attention so far is the role and impact of information and communication technologies (ICT). This section briefly gives prominence to this topic. The reason for this is obvious: information is key in reducing (distribution) costs as well as in tailoring supply chain activities to ever demanding consumer expectations and needs and, as a result, is a key competitive variable. In the information age, competition will increasingly be about the application of intangibles such as knowledge, confidence and cooperation rather than access to and control of physical assets.

Food supply chains already apply a range of ICT in order to provide individual consumers with the food they want, where and when they want it and to develop new products on the basis of consumer wishes and expectations. Food distributors offer tailor-made promotions and services through the internet on the basis of personal information and buying patterns. These trends will continue. Information technologies have an important role to play when it comes to data collection by food retailers. Nowadays, food retailers collect consumer information through, for instance, discount card systems in order to help to understand what and when their customers purchase. The extensive amount of consumer data available makes it possible to launch promotional activities – even promotions tailored to the specific demands of individual clients, to develop consumer loyalty programmes, and to improve the services offered in the supermarket. However, until now, the potential of these information technologies has not been utilised to its maximum. In general, food retailers tend to be data rich, but information poor.

Consumers, in their turn, select food providers and food products online together with a delivery mode most convenient for them, preferably direct delivery. More generally, e-commerce opens up new ways of doing transactions. Even though e-commerce is just getting off the ground, in particular in food retailing, it has the potential to broaden the scope of product sourcing to the entire globe as well as to target specific consumers. The internet also makes markets more transparent to consumers: it provides insight into the number of suppliers as well as the prices and qualities offered. Facilitated by electronic information, consumers also get access to information and virtual communities centred around all sorts of food and food-related issues ranging from special dietary needs, exotic cookery, recipes or diets to particular food brands, restaurants, community supported agriculture or production methods. With respect to the latter, an additional observation is that the food economy becomes gradually more transparent regarding characteristics and conditions of various food production processes – this is helpful for bridging the gap between the demand and supply side of the food economy.

*Information sharing between supply chain partners and a network of other suppliers and service providers are crucial to thrive and survive*

The field of food safety and information management in particular has undergone revolutionary changes in the last decade. Induced by law and liability requirements, supply chains invested heavily in electronic identification methods to make food traceable and to stay informed about animals and their well-being. Electronic identification contributes substantially to recall management and the prevention of food crises. Electronic methods, including electronic earmarks, DNA barcoding and tag injections, store information and codes about animals, their characteristics and possible certificates. As a result of these methods it is possible to trace the history of individual animals through the entire supply chain. The earmark of each animal, the ID code, remains in place in the final product. The individual animals can even be tracked through the boning plant, independent of the number of cuts in which it leaves the slaughterhouse.

Transparency and openness of food supply chains induced by ICT is also apparent when the focus is on the streamlining of logistic flows and the development of tailor-made products. In both cases, information sharing between supply chain partners and a network of other suppliers and service providers are crucial to thrive and survive. In order to optimise logistic flows and develop tailor-made products, information on demand must be captured early on. As we look to the future, we may expect innovation to take place particularly in open networks. Companies inside and outside the food supply chain will give each other access to each other's databases. The gains from access to information outside the company become greater than the gains from knowledge protection. In such a situation, the balance between controlling and sharing information shifts to the latter. In addition, the end-user might also be invited to take part in the creation of new products and services. The active involvement of consumers' ideas and creations and the utilisation of their insight and feedback, imply a reversal in the end-users' role from research object to a pro-active position where user communities are co-creators of product and service innovations. The expansion of such user-centric innovation approaches in the food economy has great potential to make the future of the food economy more consumer-oriented.

*OECD countries increasingly invest in high-tech innovation programmes which are meant to promote consumer and environmental concerns and the competitiveness of national agribusiness at the same time*

## Old wine in new bottles

Within the context of demanding consumers, an unprecedented abundance of food and food outlets, globalisation and concerns about sustainability, governments put new issues on the policy agenda, while maintaining old pre-occupations. Governments remain pre-occupied with the economic performance of their national food supply chains. In many OECD countries, the food supply chain is still a major employer. This holds true in particular for large food exporters such as Australia, Canada, France and the Netherlands. However, as the costs of logistic and information flows continue to fall and classical trade barriers become less important, OECD countries face increasing competition from low-cost competitors in e.g. South America and the former Soviet Union.

For this reason, OECD countries increasingly invest in high-tech innovation programmes which are meant to promote consumer and environmental concerns and the competitiveness of national agribusiness at the same time. The Australian Food Futures Flagship programme and the Canadian APF are good examples in this respect. The Australian programme aims at developing frontier technologies in the areas of grains, beef, aquaculture and feed (see the chapter by Loek Boonekamp *et al.*). In the 2000s, the Canadian Science and Innovation programme aimed, among other things, at enhancing supply chain co-ordination and commercialising inventions based on fundamental research (see the chapter by Tulay Yildirim and Margaret Zafiriou). The Science and Innovation program accelerated the development of a wide range of new industrial, health and nutritional products obtained from plants, animals and micro-organisms.

Food scarcity in 2007 and the subsequent surge in food prices brought another well-known policy objective back on the agenda: food security. There are still many people in the world suffering from malnutrition and hunger. Food supply in developing countries remains vulnerable to accidental contingencies in world supply, such as for instance the drought in Australia in 2006 and 2007. Such examples clearly show how safe it is to predict that food security will remain a key issue in the decades to come.

**New wine**

Even though policy objectives like economic interests and food security remain on the policy agenda, food policy is undergoing change with the arrival of new issues. Inspired by various chapters of this book, we address three of them: market concentration and competition, food quality and food standards, and, finally, consumer health and well-being.

Due to globalisation, price competition is likely to become more intense, and, paradoxically, is likely to lead to more market concentration. At the national level, concentration in food processing has been high since the 1970s and concentration in food retail has become high in the 1990s. Policymakers throughout the OECD, in particular competition authorities, carefully scrutinize supply chain transactions in order to see whether retailers or processors abuse their alleged market power. For instance, in the UK two broad investigations were launched in 2000 and 2006 to investigate retail buying behaviour apart from regular investigations targeted at specific issues such as mergers. Research has indicated that worries about market power abuse are warranted to some extent. The UK Competition Commission concluded that in a limited number of cases British supermarket chains exerted market power. However, there is no substantial evidence that food retailers or food processors wield market power and gain profits at the cost of both farmers and consumers. The OECD, in its turn, concluded that food retailers make little profit on meat and price developments at the farm, wholesale and retail level are in line with each other. What is new here is that the food market is being 'watchdogged' with respect to competition and concentration. We expect this trend to continue in the years to come.

Food quality has been on the agenda of Southern European countries such as France and Italy for some decades (see the chapter by Egizio Valceschini). The French government is actively involved in encouraging the production and consumption of regional products. This policy is aimed at products that are linked to a certain region and have traditional characteristics and a strong identity, whose production is limited and requires traditional know-how, and that do not have a close substitute. Examples of designated labels are *Appellation d'Origine Contrôlée* and the *Label Rouge*. The government supports the development of such labels and the organisation of regional networks.

*The food market is being 'watchdogged' with respect to competition and concentration; a trend, we expect to continue in the years to come*

Food safety was been placed firmly on the European policy agenda during and in the aftermath of the BSE and related veterinary crises in the 1990s and 2000s. The European Union established the General Food Law in 2005. The law assumes that the food supply chain rather than the government is responsible for food safety and that food companies are financially liable with respect to food safety. In order to meet liability requirements, all food companies – except farmers – are required to apply HACCP-quality mechanisms and to be able to track and trace food throughout the supply chain. Even though governments shift responsibility to private companies, they remain heavily involved in food safety by setting food safety standards, applying import controls and maintaining an extensive food safety system. With respect to food safety and food quality we expect that food quality in particular will evolve into an issue with new dimensions. Food quality is supposed to be increasingly interpreted in a broad sense. That is to say, food quality will be particularly defined in terms which put the emphasis on sustainable food production and consumption as well as on more healthy food supply and the encouragement of more healthy food patterns. The latter brings us directly to a third and final new issue we would like to address.

*The prognosis is that developing middle- and low-income countries are becoming the main contributors to the rise of overweight and obesity in the world*

The increased prevalence of overweight and obesity (severe overweight) is a phenomenon causing mounting concern. Driven up by sedentary lifestyles as well as the availability of a plethora of fatty, fast and irresistible favourite foods, the incidence of people with extreme overweight has risen dramatically in the last few decades. This is not only problematic because people with extreme overweight run greater risk of acquiring type-2 diabetes and cardiovascular disease – causing much harm and inconvenience to many people as well as mounting public health costs and rising mortality rates. It is also alarming because an increasing prevalence of overweight and obesity is a phenomenon that can be observed all over the world: from the United States to Kuwait and from Greece to New Zealand. Moreover, overweight is no longer a problem confined to the most advanced industrialised countries. Many developing countries also show a steep rise in the prevalence of overweight and obesity recently. The overweight epidemic has established itself particularly firmly in countries which have experienced rapid economic change in the last few decades. Therefore the prognosis is that developing middle- and low-income countries are becoming the main contributors to the rise of overweight and obesity in the world. Countries like Mexico, Brazil or China are catching up rapidly with the group of richest countries with respect to overweight and obesity percentages. Recent figures show that one third of the world's adult population is now overweight and a rise to 40% over the next 10 years is projected. In absolute numbers this means that the world is heading for a population of approximately two and a half billion people suffering from overweight. This global obesity phenomenon is rightly termed 'globesity' by the World Health Organization (WHO), and is, given its ubiquity, impossible to neglect in our reconsiderations about the food world of today and tomorrow. Next to its size and speed it is realised that overweight and obesity is fuelled by many aspects of the economic, socio-cultural, political, physical and information structures of the contemporary world. This means that one will search in vain for simple solutions or remedies to tackle the problem of overweight and obesity. Acknowledging that no single measure is adequate is a good starting point for recognising that fighting the problem of overweight and obesity is the responsibility of both governments and food business circles as well as civil society.

## New bottles

Briefly, we point towards one major divergence in government policy. Even though public regulation still proliferates, governments no longer rely on public legislation alone to achieve their objectives. Governments actively involve food companies in obtaining the objectives set in their food policies. Canada, for example, has set up value chain round tables (VCRT) in which governments and supply chain actors jointly identify bottlenecks and challenges. The VCRT provide a platform in which solutions may be developed jointly by all parties concerned. The European Union has given the key responsibility with respect to food safety to the food supply chain. Moreover, food companies develop policies with respect to social responsibility and define private standards with respect to social issues which until recently were considered to be an exclusive public responsibility.

As a result, the division between the public and the private realm has started to blur. This is particularly true as regards the relationship between public and private standards. Private food safety standards are based on public standards and *vice versa* (see the chapter by Pepijn van der Port). Moreover, private actors are involved in setting public standards, for instance in expert committees, and public officials in industry bodies are involved in developing industry wide private standards. Hence, private and public standards are very much alike and increasingly refer to each other. In reality, the body of public and private standards is the product of a public-private partnership.

## Complexity rules

The current economic downturn clearly shows the world economy's interdependence and vulnerability: for the first time since World War II, North America, Europe and Japan are all in recession at the same time. The prices of fossil fuels, agricultural commodities and other raw materials have plummeted with dazzling speed recently. Also, the world market prices for food have changed from a state that reflected scarcity one year ago to one that reflects abundance at the moment. If today's situation preludes on the years to come, we know at least one thing for certain: the issues of the food economy will become ever-growing complicated and challenging. Within this picture of the foreseeable future, the food economy as a global village with interdependent core markets dominated by a limited number of food multinationals and niche markets dominated by an increasing number of small and medium-sized enterprises, is expected to develop further. Furthermore, because trade in agricultural commodities and food products is expected to be liberalised and because multinationals increasingly source globally, changes in supply and demand conditions in one market will be more rapidly transmitted to other geographical and product markets. In addition, the food supply chain is also increasingly linked to other supply chains. Agricultural commodities are now increasingly used as an input for other products such as fuels

*If today's situation preludes on the years to come, we know at least one thing for certain: the issues of the food economy will become ever-growing complicated and challenging*

and fabrics. Finally, with the world population and standards of living still growing, environmental sustainability becomes a more important factor shaping supply and demand conditions. At the micro level, consumers put forward demands with respect to an increasing number of product characteristics including 'soft' characteristics like service, convenience and delivery, but also environmental well-being, animal welfare and fairness. The latter altruistic characteristics are also put forward by a growing number of stakeholders including NGOs and citizen groups. For both multinational and small and medium-sized companies, management of intangible assets such as knowledge and information or integrity, cooperation and trust are becoming ever more critical competition variables.

*Policy coordination with other departments and public agencies is becoming more important for food and agriculture*

Food policy is becoming more complex, not only because the context is becoming more complex, but also because the number of policy issues involved continues to grow. That is, the size of the envelope containing agriculture is expanding with respect to food policy as well. Next to classical issues like economic and trade interests and food security, new issues are evolving. To make life more complicated, many of the new issues are out of the realm of classical agricultural and food policy. This holds true, for instance, for competition issues and the fast growing issue of health. This implies that policy coordination with other departments and public agencies is becoming more important for food and agriculture. Classical topics such as economic and trade interests remain on the policy agenda, but become more complex. Until recently, agricultural policies involved relatively simple objectives with respect to production and trade positions and relatively simple instruments such as production subsidies and tariffs. Nowadays, governments in OECD countries want their agricultural and food sectors to lead in terms of productivity, technology and innovation and perform innovation and knowledge programmes. Food security remains an issue, in particular in developing countries, but is increasingly complemented by the obesity issue. Trade issues increasingly involve a range of environmental and social concerns and product standards rather than economic interests and tariffs alone.

While the number of issues on the food policy agenda grows and becomes more complicated, governments are trying to take a step back and shift responsibilities and activities to or share them with food companies and other actors including consumers. Looking to the future, we expect governments to make less use of traditional policy instruments like regulation, subsidies and tariffs and to make more use of new mechanisms like education, information provision and environmental permits. Governments will increasingly try to share the policy burden with private actors by organising private-public partnerships, roundtables, covenants or special task forces, and by shifting part of the resulting administrative burden to the private sector. Because governments share responsibilities with private parties, both companies and NGOs, private parties are likely to influence the policy agenda. On the other hand, this may very well increase the effectiveness of public policy, as governments try to commit private parties to the policy agenda. Moreover, private parties such as food companies may be expected to have a comparative advantage in implementing policies.

The introductory chapter of this book begins with a quote from Douglas Southgate *et al.* We would like to close this concluding chapter by citing another sentence from *The World Food Economy*: 'The only safe predictions that can be made about the twenty-first century are that age-old challenges to the food economy will persist and that novel problems [or: issues – to use the vocabulary of the subtitle of this book] will emerge.' (Southgate *et al.*, 2007: 9)

# References

## Expanding the size of the envelope that contains agriculture

Kinsey, J.D. (2001) The New Food Economy: Consumers, Farms, Pharms, and Science. *American Journal of Agricultural Economics*, 83, pp. 1113-1130.

Korthals, M. (2004) *Before Dinner: Philosophy and Ethics of Food*. Dordrecht: Springer.

Lang, T. and Heasman, M. (2004) *Food Wars: The Global Battle for Mouths, Minds and Markets*. London: Earthscan.

Lawrence, F. (2004) *Not on the Label: What Really Goes Into the Food on Your Plate*. London: Penguin Books.

Lawrence, F. (2008) *Eat Your Heart Out: Why the Food Business is Bad for the Planet and Your Health*. London: Penguin Books.

Patel, R. (2007) *Stuffed and Starved: Markets, Power and the Hidden Battle for the World's Food System*. London: Portobello Books.

Petrini, C. (2007) *Slow Food Nation: Why Our Food Should be Good, Clean and Fair*. New York: Rizzoli Ex Libris.

Pollan, M. (2006) *The Omnivore's Dilemma: The Search For a Perfect Meal in a Fast-Food World*. London: Bloomsbury.

Pollan, M. (2008) *In Defence of Food: An Eater's Manifesto*. New York: Penguin Press.

Schlosser, E. (2001) *Fast Food Nation: The Dark Side of the All-American Meal*. Boston: Houghton Mifflin Company.

Singer, P. and J. Mason (2006) *The Way We Eat: Why Our Food Choices Matter*. Emmaus: Rodale Books.

Southgate, D., D.H. Graham and L. Tweeten (2007) *The World Food Economy*. Oxford: Blackwell Publishing.

Stiglitz, J.E. (2006) *Making Globalization Work*. New York: W.W. Norton.

Weis, T. (2007) *The Global Food Economy: The Battle for the Future of Food*. London: Zed Books.

Wilk, R. (2006) From Wild Weeds to Artisanal Cheese. In: R. Wilk (Ed.) *Fast Food/Slow Food: The Cultural Economy of the Global Food System*. Lanham: Altamira Press, pp. 13-27.

## Globalisation in the food industry

Baumol, W.J., J.C. Panzar and R.D. Willig (1982) *Contestable Markets and the Theory of Market Structure*, New York: Harcourt Brace Jovanovich.

Belcher, K., J. Nolan and P.W.B. Phillips (2005) Genetically Modified Crops and Agricultural Landscapes: Spatial Patterns of Contamination. *Ecological Economics*, 53, pp. 387-401.

Bolling, C. and M. Gehlhar (2005) Global Food Manufacturing Reorients to Meet New Demands. In A. Regmi and M. Gehlhar (Eds.) *New Directions in Global Food Markets*. Electronic report from the Economic Research Service of the United States Department of Agriculture, Agriculture Information Bulletin Number 794 (www.ers.usda.gov).

Boone, C., G.R. Carroll and A. van Witteloostuijn (2002) Resource Distributions and Market Partitioning: Dutch Daily Newspapers, 1968 to 1994. *American Sociological Review*, 67, pp. 408-431.

Boone, C. and A. van Witteloostuijn (2004) Towards a Unified Theory of Market Partitioning: Integrating Resource Partitioning and Sunk Cost Theories of Dual Market Structures. *Industrial and Corporate Change*, 13, pp. 701-726.

Bordo, M.D., A.M. Taylor and J.G. Williamson (Eds.) (2003) *Globalization in Historical Perspective*. Chicago: Chicago University Press.

Brakman, S., H. Garretsen, C. van Marrewijk and A. van Witteloostuijn (2006) *Nations and Firms in the Global Economy: An Introduction into International Economics and Business*, Cambridge: Cambridge University Press.

Carroll, G.R. and A. Swaminathan. (2000) Why the Microbrewery Movement?: Organizational Dynamics of Resource Partitioning in the US Brewing Industry. *American Journal of Sociology*, 106, pp. 715-762.

Cioffi, A. and C. dell'Aquila (2004) The Effects of Trade Policies for Fresh Fruit and Vegetables of the European Union. *Food Policy*, 29, pp. 169-185.

Dikova, D. and A. van Witteloostuijn (2008) Acquisition versus Greenfield Foreign Entry: Diversification Mode Choice in Central and Eastern Europe. *Journal of International Business Studies*, 38, pp. 1013-1033.

Feenstra, R.C. (2004) *Advanced International Trade*. Princeton: Princeton University Press.

Friedman, T.L. (2006) *The World is Flat: A Brief History of the Twenty-First Century*. New York: Farrar, Straus and Giroux.

Gow, H.R. and J.F.M. Swinnen (1998) Up- and Downstream Restructuring, Foreign Direct Investment, and Hold-Up Problems in Agricultural Transition. *European Review of Agricultural Economics*, 25, pp. 331-350.

Hobbs, J.E. and W.A. Kerr (2006) Consumer Information, Labelling and International Trade in Agri-Food Products. *Food Policy*, 31, pp. 78-89.

Krugman, P (1995) Growing World Trade: Causes and Consequences. *Brooking Papers on Economic Activity*, 1, pp. 327-377.

Pinstrup-Andersen, P. (2000) Food Policy Research for Developing Countries: Emerging Issues and Unfinished Business. *Food Policy*, 25, pp. 125-141.

Popkin, B.M. (2006) Technology, Transport, Globalisation and the Nutrition Food Policy. *Food Policy*, 31, pp. 554-569.

Rae, A. and T. Josling (2003) Processed Food Trade and Developing Countries: Protection and Trade Liberalisation. *Food Policy*, 28, pp. 147-166.

Regmi, A. and M. Gehlhar (Eds) (2005) *New Directions in Global Food Markets*. Electronic report from the Economic Research Service of the United States Department of Agriculture, Agriculture Information Bulletin Number 794 (www.ers.usda.gov).

Sorge, A.M. (2005) *The Global and the Local: Understanding the Dialectics of Business Systems*. Oxford: Oxford University Press.

Sutton, J. (1991) *Sunk Costs and Market Structure: Price Competition, Advertising and the Evolution of Concentration*. Cambridge: MIT Press.

Traill, B. (1997) Globalisation in Food Industries. *European Review of Agricultural Economics*, 24, pp. 390-410.

Trotter, B. and A. Gordon (2000) Charting Change in Official Assistance to Agriculture. *Food Policy*, 25, pp. 115-124.

Van Witteloostuijn, A. and C. Boone (2006) A Resource-Based Theory of Market Structure and Organisational Form. *Academy of Management Review*, 31, pp. 409-426.

Winters, L.A. (2005) The European Agricultural Trade Policies and Poverty. *European Review of Agricultural Economics*, 32, pp. 319-346.

## The food economy of today and tomorrow

Blonigen, B.A. (2005) A Review of the Empirical Literature on FDI Determinants. Eugene: University of Oregon, mimeo.

ERS (2005) *New Directions in Global Food Markets*. ERS: Agriculture Information Bulletin Number 794.

Fulponi, L. (2007) The Globalisation of Private Standards and the Agri-Food System. In: J.F.M. Swinnen (Ed.) *Global Supply Chains, Standards and the Poor: How the Globalisation of Food Systems and Standards Affects Rural Development and Poverty*. Wallingford: CABI.

Henson S., R. Loader, A. Swinbank and M. Bredahl (2004) How Developing Countries View the Impact of Sanitary and Phytosanitary Measures on Agricultural Exports. In: M.D. Ingco and L.A. Winters (Eds.) *Agriculture and the New Trade Agenda: Creating a Global Trading Environment for Development*, Cambridge: Cambridge University Press, pp. 359-375.

Hertel T., K. Anderson, J. Francois and W. Martin (2004) The Global and Regional Effects of Liberalizing Agriculture and Other Trade in the New Round. In: M.D. Ingco and L.A. Winters (Eds.) *Agriculture and the New Trade Agenda: Creating a Global Trading Environment for Development*. Cambridge: Cambridge University Press, pp. 221-244.

Jacobs, K. (2007) 2016: The Future Value Chain. Paper presented ad the OECD/NL Conference on the Future of the Food Economy, 18-19 October 2007, The Hague.

Knowles, M. (2007) Future Perceptions of Food – European Beverage Industry 2030. Paper presented at the Conference Perspectives for Food 2030, 17-18 October 2007, Brussels.

LEI (2009) *De Agrarische Sector in Nederland naar 2020: Perspectieven en Onzekerheden*. Den Haag: LEI Wageningen UR.

OECD (2006) *Linkages between Foreign Direct Investment, Trade and Trade Policy: An Economic Analysis with Application to the Food Sector*. Paris: Organisation for Economic Cooperation and Development.

OECD/FAO (2007) *OECD-FAO Agricultural Outlook: 2007-2016*. Paris: Organisation for Economic Cooperation and Development.

Pyke, F., G. Becattini and W. Sengenberger (Eds.) (1990) *Industrial Districts and Interfirm Co-operation in Italy*. Geneva: International Institute for Labour Studies.

Stanton, G. (2004) A Review of the Operation of the Agreement on Sanitary and Phytosanitary Measures. In: M.D. Ingco and L.A. Winters (Eds.) *Agriculture and the New Trade Agenda: Creating a Global Trading Environment for Development*. Cambridge: Cambridge University Press, pp. 101-110.

The Food Economy

Sutton, J. (1991) *Sunk Costs and Market Structure: Price Competition, Advertising and the Evolution of Concentration*. Cambridge: MIT Press.

Sutton, J. (2003) Understanding the Rise in Global Concentration in the Agri-Food Sector: A Background Paper. Paper presented at the OECD Conference on Changing Dimensions of the Food Economy, 6-7 Februari 2003, The Hague.

Swinnen, J.F.M. (Ed.) (2007) *Global Supply Chains, Standards and the Poor: How the Globalisation of Food Systems and Standards Affects Rural Development and Poverty*. Wallingford: CABI.

Vindigni G., P. Nijkamp, G. Carra and Iuri Peri (2006) Organisational Success Factors in Local Agri-Food Industries. In: T. De Noronha Vaz, E.J. Morgan and P. Nijkamp (Eds.) *The New European Rurality: Strategies for Small Firms*. Aldershot: Ashgate, pp. 107-128.

## The biofuels boom

Alexander, C. and C. Hurt (2007) Biofuels and Their Impact on Food Prices. Bioenergy, Purdue Extension, ID-346-W., http://www.ces.purdue.edu/extmedia/ID/ID-346-W.pdf.

Birur, D.K., T.W. Hertel and W.E. Tyner (2007) *Impact of Biofuel Production on World Agricultural Markets: A Computable General Equilibrium Analysis*. GTAP Working Paper.

Commission of European Communities (2003) Directive 2003/30/EC of the European Parliament and of the Council of 8 May 2003 on the Promotion of the Use of Biofuels or Other Renewable Fuels for Transport, *Official Journal of the European Union*, L123/42-46, http://ec.europa.eu/energy/res/legislation/doc/biofuels/en_final.pdf.

FAPRI (2007) US and World Agricultural Outlook. Iowa State University: Food and Agricultural Policy Research Institute.

Hertel, T.W., H. Lee, S. Rose and B. Sohngen (2008) Modeling Land-use Related Greenhouse Gas Sources and Sinks and their Mitigation Potential. In: T. Hertel, S. Rose and R. Tol (Eds.) *Economic Analysis of Land Use in Global Climate Change Policy*. London: Routledge.

Tokgoz, S., A. Elobeid, J.F. Fabiosa, D.J. Hayes, B.A. Babcock, T.-H. Yu, F. Dong, C.E. Hart and J.C. Beghin (2007) Emerging Biofuels: Outlook of Effects on US Grain, Oilseed, and Livestock Markets. Staff report 07-SR 101, Iowa State University: Center for Agricultural and rural Development, http://www.card.iastate.edu/publications/synopsis.aspx?id=1050

Tyner W.E. and F. Taheripour (2007) Future Biofuels Policy Alternatives. Paper presented at the Biofuels, Food & Feed Tradeoffs Conference Organized by the Farm Foundation and USDA, St. Louis, Missouri, April 12-13.

## Informing consumers

AGENDA (2004) Consuming for Good? The Role of Consumers in Driving Responsible Business. With the Support of the Scottish Consumer Council.

Alter Eco (2005) 2000-2005 Les Consommateurs Français et Le Commerce Equitable. http://www.alterecosud.com/pdf/etude consommateurs complete 2005.pdf

Berens, G. (2006) Creating Consumer Confidence in Corporate Social Responsibility: How to Communicate about CSR? Rotterdam: RSM Erasmus University, unpublished manuscript.

Collinson, C. (2001) *The Business Cost of Ethical Supply Chain Management: Kenya's Flower Industry Case Study*. Chatham: Natural Resources Institute.

Cowe, R. and S. Williams (2000) *Who are the Ethical Consumers?* Manchester: The Co-operative Bank Manchester.

Dawkins, J. and S. Lewis (2003) CSR in Stakeholder Expectations and their Implications for Company Strategy. *Journal of Business Ethics*, 44, pp.185-193.

Doane, D. (2005) The Myth of Corporate Social Responsibility. *Stanford Social Innovation Review*, Fall, pp. 23-29.

GlobeScan (2005) Corporate Social Responsibility Monitor 2004, www.globescan.com

Herpen, E. van, J.M.E. Pennings and M. Meulenberg (2003) Consumers' Evaluations of Socially Responsible Activities in Retailing, mimeo

Imug (2003) Themenspot Verbraucher und Corporate Social Responsibility: Ergebnisse einer bundesweiten repräsentativen imug-Mehrthemenumfrage. Hannover: Institut für Markt-Umwelt-Gesellschaft e.V.

Ipsos Reid (2003) Canadian Champion Good Corporate Citizens, www.ipsos-na.com/news/pressrelease.cfm?id=1899

Keller, K.L. and D.A. Aaker (1998) The Impact of Corporate Marketing on a Company's Brand Extensions. *Corporate Reputation Review*, 1, pp. 356-378.

KPMG (2005) *International Survey on Corporate Responsibility Reporting 2005*. Amsterdam: KPMG.

Maronick, T.J. and J.C. Andrews (1999) The Role of Qualifying Language on Consumer Perceptions of Environmental Claims. *Journal of Consumer Affairs*, 33, pp. 297-320.

Miele M. and V. Parisi (1998) *Consumer Concerns about Animal Welfare and the Impact on Food Choice: Literature Review and Policy Aspects*. Pisa: Department of Agricultural Economics, University of Pisa.

Mohr, L.A. and D.J. Webb (2005) The Effects of Corporate Social Responsibility and Price on Consumer Responses. *Journal of Consumer Affairs*, 39, pp. 121-147.

MORI (2000) The First Ever European Survey of Consumer Attitudes Towards Corporate Social Responsibility. Brussels: CSR Europe.

MORI (2003) The Public's Views of Corporate Responsibility. London.

Muldoon, J. and P. Scott (2005) Creating the International Standard for the Trade in Live Reef Food Fish, APEC Fisheries Working Group.

OECD (2006) *Final Report on Private Standards and the Shaping of the Agro-food System*. Paris: Organisation for Economic Cooperation and Development.

Poncibò, C. (2007) Private Certification Schemes as Consumer Protection: A Viable Supplement to Regulation in Europe? *International Journal of Consumer Studies*, 31, pp. 650-661.

Swaen, V. and J. Vanhamme (2004) See How 'Good' We Are: The Dangers of Using Corporate Social Activities in Communication Campaigns. *Advances in Consumer Research*, 31, pp. 302-313.

UNEP (2005) The Trade and Environment Effects of Ecolabels: Assessment and Response, http://www.unep.ch/etb/publications/Ecolabelpap141005f.pdf

Werther, W.B. and D. Chandler (2005) Strategic Corporate Social Responsibility as Global Brand Insurance. *Business Horizons*, 48, pp. 317-324.

Zadek, S., S. Lingayah and M. Forstater (1998) *Social Labels: Tools for Ethical Trade*. Brussels: New Economics Foundation for the European Commission.

## The interplay between private and public food safety standards

Barton, J.H., J.L. Goldstein, T.E. Josling and R.H. Steinberg (2006) *The Evolution of the Trading Regime: Politics, Law and Economics of the GATT and the WTO*. Princeton: Princeton University Press.

Brunsson, N., B. Jacobsson and Associates (2002) *A World of Standards*. Oxford: Oxford University Press.

Cheit, R.A. (1990) *Setting Safety Standards: Regulation in the Public and Private Sectors*. Berkely: University of California Press.

EU (2002) Regulation of the European Parlement and of the Council of 28 January 2002 laying down the general principles and requirements of food law, establishing the European Food Safety Authority and laying down procedures in matters of food safety.

EU (2004) EU Regulation (EC) No 852/2004 of the European Parliament and of the Council of 29 April 2004, on the hygiene of foodstuffs.

EU (2005) Regulation (EC) No 183/2005 of the European Parlement and Council of the European Union of 12 January 2005 laying down requirements for feed hygiene.

EU (2007) Commision working staff report. Annex by the Report from the Commission to the European Parliament and the council on existing legal provisions, systems and practices in the Member States and at Community level relating to liability in the food and feed sectors and on feasible systems for financial guarantees in the feed sector at Community level in accordance with Article 8 of Regulation (EC) No 183/2005 of the European Parliament and of the Council of 12 January 2005 laying down requirements for feed hygiene.

EU/DG SANCO (2006) Guidance Document on Key Questions Related to Import Requirements and the New Rules on Food Hygiene and Official Food Controls.

Hallstrom, K.T. (2004) *Organizing International Standardization: ISO and the IASC in Quest of Authority*. Cheltenham: Edward Elgar.

Hulebak, K.L. and W. Schlosser (2002) Hazard Analysis and Critical Control Point (HACCP) History and Conceptual Overview. *Risk Analysis*, 22, pp. 547-552.

Porter, T. and K. Ronit (2006) Self-Regulation as Policy Process: The Multiple and Criss-Crossing Stages of Private Rule-Making. *Policy Sciences*, 39, pp. 41-72.

Smith, D.F. and J. Phillips (Eds.) (2000) *Food, Science, Policy and Regulation in the Twentieth Century: International and Comparitive Perspectives*. London: Routledge.

WTO (2007) Private standards and the SPS agreement: Background Note by the Secretariat of the SPS committee. Geneva: WTO Committee on Sanitary and Phytosanitary Measures.

## Making the livestock sector more sustainable

Steinfeld, H., P. Gerber, T. Wassenaar, V. Castel, M. Rosales and C. de Haan (2006) *Livestock's Long Shadow: Environmental Issues and Options*. Rome: Food and Agricultural Organization.

## Food policy in practice

Borraz, O. (2007) Governing Standards: The Rise of Standardization Processes in France and in the EU. *Governance*, 20, pp. 57-84.

Ménard, C. and E. Valceschini (2005) News Institutions for Governing the Agri-food Industry. *European Review of Agricultural Economics*, 32, pp. 421-440.

North, D.C. (1990) *Institutions, Institutional Change and Economic Performance*. Cambridge: Cambridge University Press

## Food for thought

OECD (2005) Competition and Regulation in Agriculture: Monopsony Buying and Joint Selling. Unpublished report, DAF/COMP 44. Paris: Organisation for Economic Cooperation and Development.

OECD (2006) *Supermarkets and the Meat Supply Chain: The Economic Impact of Food Retail on Farmers, Processors and Consumers*. Paris: Organisation for Economic Cooperation and Development.

OECD (2006b) *Final Report on Private Standards and the Shaping of the Agro-Food System*. Paris: Organisation for Economic Cooperation and Development.

OECD (2007) *Private Standard Schemes and Developing Country Access to Global Value Chains: Challenges and Opportunities Emerging from Four Case Studies*. Paris: Organisation for Economic Cooperation and Development.

Regina, A., A. Bird, D. Topping, S. Bowden, J. Freeman, T. Barsby, B. Kosar-Hashemi, Z. Li, S. Rahman and M. Morell (2006) High-amylose Wheat Generated by RNA Interference Improves Indices of Large-bowel Health in Rats. *Proceedings of the National Academy of Sciences of the USA*, 103, pp. 3546-3551.

## Anticipating the future of the food economy

Heller, Z. (2008) *The Believers*. London: Fig Tree.

Southgate, D., D.H. Graham and L. Tweeten (2007) *The World Food Economy*. Oxford: Blackwell Publishing.

# Contributors

*Dileep Birur* is graduate research assistant in the Department of Agricultural Economics at Purdue University (Indiana, USA)

*Loek Boonekamp* is former head of the Agri-food Trade and Markets Division, Trade and Agriculture Directorate at the OECD (Paris, France)

*Frank Bunte* is senior researcher at the Agricultural Economics Research Institute – LEI Wageningen UR (The Hague, The Netherlands)

*Hans Dagevos* is senior researcher at the Agricultural Economics Research Institute – LEI Wageningen UR (The Hague, The Netherlands)

*Barbara Fliess* is senior analyst at the Trade and Agriculture Directorate of the OECD (Paris, France)

*Thomas Hertel* is professor in the Department of Agricultural Economics at Purdue University (Indiana, USA) and executive director of the Global Trade Analysis Project

*Bruce Lee* is director of the Food Futures Flagship at CSIRO (North Ryde NSW, Australia)

*Pepijn van de Port* is associate professor at the Faculty of Social Sciences at the Free University (Amsterdam, The Netherlands)

*Henning Steinfeld* is chief of the Livestock Information, Sector analysis and Policy Branch, Animal Production and Health Division at FAO (Rome, Italy)

*Wallace Tyner* is professor in the Department of Agricultural Economics at Purdue University (Indiana, USA)

*Egizio Valceschini* is researcher at INRA-DARESE (Paris, France)

*Gérard Viatte* is former director of the former Food, Agriculture and Fisheries Directorate at the OECD (Paris, France)

*Arjen van Witteloostuijn* is professor at the University of Antwerp (Belgium) and at the Utrecht School of Economics, Utrecht University (The Netherlands)

*Tulay Yildirim* is director of the Economic and Industry Analysis Division at the Canadian Department of Agriculture and Agri-food (Ottawa, Canada)

*Margaret Zafiriou* is chief Agri-food Chain Analysis at the Canadian Department of Agriculture and Agri-food (Ottawa, Canada)